Herausgeber: Tim Goydke & Günter Koch

Umschlaggestaltung: Sebastian Büsching Illustration und Grafik-Design

Verlag & Druck: tredition GmbH, Halenreie 40-44, 22359 Hamburg

978-3-347-18431-2 (Paperback)
978-3-347-18432-9 (Hardcover)
978-3-347-18433-6 (e-Book)

Bibliografische Information der Deutschen Nationalbibliothek:
Die Deutsche Nationalbibliothek verzeichnet diese Publikation in der Deutschen Nationalbibliografie; detaillierte bibliografische Daten sind im Internet über http://dnb.d-nb.de abrufbar.

Kontakt:
Prof. Dr. Tim Goydke
Hochschule Bremen
Langemarckstr. 113 | D-28199 Bremen
Tel.: +49 421 5905-4133 | E-Mail: tim.goydke@hs-bremen.de

# Economy for the Common Good - A Common Standard for a Pluralist World?

**Tim Goydke and Günter Koch (eds.)**

# Table of Content

# An Economy for the Common Good Standard for a Pluralist World?

*Tim Goydke and Günter Koch*

## 1. Introduction

In late 2019 the first international scientific conference on the Economy for the Common Good was organized by the School of Graduate and Professional Studies (Institut für Wissenschaftliche Weiterbildung) of Hochschule Bremen – City University of Applied Sciences and the Research Council of the Economy for the Common Good (Forschungsverein der Gemeinwohlökonomie e.V.), with participants from Germany, Austria, Belgium, Brazil, Mexico, the Netherlands, and the UK.

The conference gave a first comprehensive survey which type of projects under the philosophical umbrella of the ECG are *en route*, as well on the deficiencies still to be bridged in order to emancipate the ECG and its instruments to become fully approbated in the political, economic and business arena. The promoters of the ECG by their contributions and through the intense discussions became aware, that there still exist deficiencies both in the methodology as well as with regard to the wider acceptance in politics and in business. It opened the opportunity to identify strengths and weaknesses of the current ECG / CGBS model and its implementations thus generating ideas how the ECG project must be furthered in order to find wider acceptance. In this sense, this report incentivises future research contributing to new models of economic and societal design.

This conference for the first time brought together scientists mainly from the German speaking ECG community engaged in a **variety of disciplines** such as economics, sociology, law, natural sciences, informatics, philosophy and theology. This collection makes evident, that future models of economy science and of economy in general need to include more of methodological knowledge than is summarized in one traditional discipline. An insight gained so far is that the debate opened by the conference will give **impulses to the formation of new economic models** by exercising transdisciplinary research with the aim to integrate the seemingly diverse aspects addressed in this conference. This discovery on the one hand will fuel the debate in positioning the ECG within the landscape of the many economic models in discourse, and, on the other hand, we can expect that the theoretical foundation of the ECG and related models will be strengthened.

Up to today, the contributions assembled in this publication and the discussions on it lead to a first conclusion which is, that the ECG, its movement and its concrete projects in applying the CGBS offer a wide sample of processes in implementing and anchoring the ECG in real settings, as are in companies and public administrations. Investigating into these projects by means of well-designed research conforming to standards of good sociological and organisational science rules, it opens the entry door for next phase research expectedly ending in **sound theory building** in favour of the ECG and thereby also in contributing to the **convergency in CSR standards** as a first level achievement, then subsequently to approach to "coagulate" a theory of an alternative model of economy devoted to include the common good as well as "the good life" for all, especially overcoming the outdated reference to the GDP.

## 2. Background

The idea of the common good is as old as the Classical Civilization. In the Greek antiquity, philosophers like Aristotle (384 – 322 BC) considered the political good as the just which in turn served the common good. In the 6th century the term "res communis" was introduced into Roman civil law, encompassing resources that belongs to all and could be enjoyed by everyone, i.e. air, waters, the sea (Barresi 2012). The "Economy for the Common Good" (ECG) movement builts on the idea of the common good and aims to link economic activity more closely with basic democratic values and social and ecological requirements. The ECG movement started in 2010 with the publication of the first edition of the book "Gemeinwohl-Ökonomie" (Economy for the Common Good) by the Austrian activist and author Christian Felber (Felber 2010). Up until today, more than 2,000 companies, mainly small and medium-sized enterprises (SMEs), have been registered as supporters and some hundred companies have already prepared or are currently preparing an CGBS on a voluntary basis. The movement spread from the German-speaking countries to other countries, especially to Italy, Spain, the Netherlands and Latin America. The ECG also advocates the idea that a change in the incentive structure could lead to a general paradigm shift, e.g. companies with an outstanding ECG score could in future benefit from lower taxes, easier access to grants or credits, or preference in public procurement (Heidbrink et al. 2018).

In 2011, a first version of the common good balance sheet (CGBS) was presented by a group of Austrian entrepreneurs. Central to the CGBS is that it broadens the focus and, instead of focussing on financial indicators alone, asks how a company contributes to the implementation of the four value categories "human dignity", "solidarity and justice", "ecological sustainability" and "transparency and co-determination" (GWÖ 2017). These categories are than linked to five stakeholder groups, resulting in a matrix of 20 topics, which are backed by a set of questions and requirements. With a scoring system of up to 1,000 points in total, the 20 subject areas are assessed by external auditors. Companies earn points if their performance exceeds a defined minimum standard. Additionally, points can be deducted for negative aspects, such as a lack of anti-corruption measures or violations of environmental regulations. The verification can be performed either through peer to peer procedure (similar to benchmarking) or by an external audit (approved auditors). The CGBS is constantly reviewed and further developed based on the feedback from the auditors and the audited companies (ibid.).

## 3. Critics

Despite the fast growing acceptance of the ECG among especially SMEs, NGOs, and within the civil society, criticism from the academia is also apparent. The critics focus in particular on the lacking scientific foundation of the model and a sound statistical validation of the CGBS. Whereas a number of empirical studies has already focussed on the effects of shareholder-orientation and profit-maximization on corporations and employees, very few investigates the practical effects of an orientation towards the common good on a corporate level until recently. Similarly, Corporate Social Responsibility (CSR) has been subject of extensive research (e.g. Nelson 2004; Ruggie 2000), but only very few scientific publications have taken the ECG into focus (e.g. Heidbrink et al. 2018). However, in the last 2-3 years several conceptual and empirical works have tried to close this gap.

## 4. Related Approaches

The ECG makes reference to a number of well-grounded and widely accepted economic theories and models. Moreover, recent seminal work has proven the connectivity with other alternative approaches.

The ECG approach is in line with approaches that underline the need to integrate economic, social and environmental aspects into management (e.g. Dyllick & Hockerts, 2002; Johnson & Schaltegger, 2016; Joyce & Paquin, 2016). Similar to the **Triple Bottom Line (TBL)** approach (Elkington, 1997), the ECG is proposing an alternative to the classical neoliberal model by highlighting the need for a better balance between economic, social and environmental outcomes. Different to the TBL, the ECG model emphasizes more clearly the potential contribution of a business entity to the common good and the importance of cooperation instead of competition and profit maximization. The social dimension in the ECG model values more universal and basic principles of human rights, more specifically, human dignity, solidarity and social justice, ecological sustainability, and democratic participation and transparency (Felber, 2015).

The ECG has furthermore much in common with the **Shared Value Approach** (Porter & Kramer, 2006) which is based on the assumption that value has both an economic and social dimension. While the creation of value is well established as a concept in management, societal issues are rarely analyzed by corporations so far, obscuring the link between societal and economic progress. However, different to the SVA, the ECG prefers cooperation over competition and it considers profit und economic value creation not as a goal in itself but as a mean to generate social and environmental value, thus, contributing to the common good.

The ECG, and especially the CGBS suggests an organizational behaviour model based on the **Stakeholder Theory** (Freeman, 1984). The CGBS is based on a matrix which combines the business activities of the organization with its different stakeholders (suppliers, owners, equity and financial service providers, employees, customers, and business partners and social environment) and measures the degree of contribution to the common good. Moreover, the ECG model also incorporates a multi-stakeholders approach suggesting that value should be distributed among the different stakeholders (internal and external to the organization).

Giesenbauer & Müller-Christ (2018) have shown that the ECG approach can be matched with the **Sustainable Development Goals** (see: GAIA Sonderheft 2019: Sustainable Economy Perspectives of Change; GAIA 02/2019 Research for Sustainable Development Goals) and a ECG study group is currently working on a practical guide for companies.

The widely committed engagements and projects by political, societal and economic institutions in implementing the **Sustainable Development Goals** also challenges the ECG community in finding out how such high aiming goals as are the SDGs can be achieved in practice. The ECG and its key tool, the common good balance sheet (CGBS), offers a methodological instrument complementary to other CSR reporting in order to both implement and to analyse the (partial) fulfilment of SDG requirements in practice. The insight developed in the conference gained is that the CGBS not only fulfils current requirements of CSR reports, in several aspects it even surpasses such existing standards.

Key arguments of opponents to the ECG approach are that it lacks democratic legitimation in the sense that it is not converging towards a legal obligation, or that it is too normative and prescriptive thus opposing liberal principles (Meynhardt 2017). Although sympathetic with the general ideas of the ECG, other authors like Schumeister (2014) make the point, that the ECG as promoted in its 1st issue by Christian Felber (Felber 2010) lacks the embedding in historical context and in the overall current discussion on the future of economic models. (Meanwhile, Felber in his latest book (Felber 2019) took this criticism and contrasted the ECG approach versus other economic concepts).

## 6. Structure of the Book

The chapters of this publications were prepared in the spirit described above. This book includes nine outstanding contributions.

We put **Bernd Fittkau**'s contribution at the beginning, because he gave a broad overview on the topics of our conference, as well as on the connections to other projects and thoughts in the domain of the Economy of the Common Good. The original version of his contribution was by far more extensive than the one presented in this volume, i.e. the article reproduced here and edited by Günter Koch reduced it to set the key themes of our conference. What is fascinating about his approach is that he discusses the core concern of the Economy for the Common Good under the aspect of "mental sustainability" and for this purpose - quasi as a spotlight - he elaborates four aspects, the titles of which are: (1) From constant growth to balance, (2) From need orientation to value orientation, (3) From the specialists' view to a view towards global orientation, (4) From a strategy of egocentric "bread and games" policy towards an economy of sound ecosystems. At the end, Bernd Fittkau presented his lecture with a wink and irony, reporting on the strange incident of the elimination of the appreciation of Christian Felber as an alternative economist in an Austrian textbook. Without being able to discuss this event in depth, by this he addressed a point of importance, namely the relationship of orthodox economists to the still little scientifically consolidated movement of Common Good Economics, which is to be judged as anything but conciliatory.

**Daniel Dahm** outlines in his contribution the basic principles of a new, sustainable and regenerative economy and provides a benchmark for sustainability: the Sustainability Zeroline. Daniel Dahm clarifies that the regeneration and strengthening of biological diversity, fertility and its potentiality, are preconditions for the carrying capacity of the planetary habitats and thus for the sustainability of the Homo sapiens.

With the re-evaluation of economic practices and processes along their (positive as well as negative) effects on the material and immaterial foundations of life in the biogeosphere and anthroposphere, the externalizations of benefits into the planetary life system including humans would become the driving force for economic action. With this, Dahm creates a methodological basis for a regenerative economy and thus for the reorientation of economic activities along ecological principles as diversity and difference, freedom and solidarity in answer to the climatic-ecological and humanitarian-cultural challenges of humanity.

The contribution of **Maria Angelica Jung Marques, Jamile Sabatini Marques, Blanca C. Garcia, and Tatiana Tucunduva Philippi Cortese** intends to answer the research question whether and how the commons theory may contribute to a better understanding of the field of Knowledge-Based Development (KBD). Based on an analysis of the similarities and differences between the KBD theory and the Commons theory, the authors come to the conclusion that is necessary to broaden the discussion and studies on the contribution of commons and new commons to KBD and future research that may characterize commons as drivers of knowledge-based development.

**Elly Rijnierse** explores the dynamics of competing governance structures in the Sahel in the context of climate change and conflict. She suggests that a Universal Social Contract as a common goal may provide a direction to create a pathway to the Economy of the Common Good. While extrapolating from the Sahel, Elly Rijnierse concludes that ecosystems, including expanding cities that depend on them, may become the centre pieces of social organisation and environmental management, to be achieved through time and place specific strategies. This requires a firm enhancement of the organisation of the 'Plural Sector', including its legal anchoring in participatory processes. The role of the State is to shift from an orchestrating role over its own territory to a facilitating role, serving multiple ecosystems within or transcending its territory.

In their contribution **Anna Deparnay-Grunenberg and Bianca Llerandi** aim at pointing out the gaps in research that need to be filled in order to impact the socio-ecological trans-formation on the political agenda. The chapter also gives an outlook on the possibilities presented for a new Common Agricultural Policy (CAP). The CAP is in a transitional phase and therefore presents a window of opportunity to be reconceptualized. A new CAP that distributes subventions based on criteria from ECG and related approaches would be a milestone for social and ecological sustainability in the field. While the awareness for a need for a more sustainable economy has risen and approaches such as the Economy for the Common Good (ECG) and related theories have gained interest, we are lacking a common framework that bundles such approaches and thus strengthens them.

**Tim Goydke** introduces, frames, and critically discuss the approach of the International Graduate Center (IGC), Bremen City University of Applied Sciences, Germany, has chosen to integrate sustainability into its operation and teaching by applying a holistic model which is based on the idea of the Economy for the Common Good (ECG). The chapter puts the ECG framework in relation to other methods to implement and assess sustainability in higher education, especially in business schools, and will outline the impact it can have on major stakeholder groups like students, faculty, staff, and the way in which organisational change can occur and lead to improved accountability and changes in sustainability performance in a B-school setting.

**Nathali Jänicke** investigates where connecting points exist between the ecological sustainability of the common good balance sheet and the environmental planning of the management system, especially to the international environmental management system in accordance with ISO 14001:2015. Both concepts use the stakeholder approach and aim to reduce environmental impact. With the understanding of the organization and its context, especially the internal and external issues, there are further links to the common good balance sheet. The result of this investigation are the commonalities and differences between the two concepts in order to derive recommendations for the introduction of the common good balance sheet in the context of ecological sustainability.

When practically working towards the common good and cooperation as value above profit-orientation and competition, the transformation of conventional economic processes requires engineering support. In his study, **Christian Stary** challenges business process modelling to represent both, conventional and ECG structures and processes, based on existing field studies. Process models allow capturing the behaviour of relevant actors and their contextual relationships from an organizational perspective. Once they can be executed, they enable interactive experiencing of ECG transformation approaches. In this way, digital processes can be utilized to make transparent fundamental ECG principles, and to simulate transformation designs before introducing them in everyday life.

**Johannes Panhofer** discusses the similarities and differences of the position of Pope Francis to the approach of the ECG. With his so-called encyclical on environment "Laudato Si" Pope Francis has received great respect and wide approval - far beyond the Catholic Church. In "care for our common home" he calls for a new kind of economy, because: "This economy kills!" Pope Francis criticises the "globalization of the technocratic paradigm". It urgently needs a different way of life that overcomes the self-destructing mechanisms of the market and that guides us to a "bold cultural revolution". Pope Francis appeals to the searching people: "Your universities, companies and organizations should become 'wellsprings of hope' ". And he encourages the young entrepreneurs: "I also ask you to be the main actor of this change ..." What could be the contribution of spiritual and religious traditions to a "global common welfare"?

Finally, **Christian Harant** provides an account on how the conferences was designed in an innovative way using up-to date formats to encourage dialogue and response and limiting standard format sessions to a minimum.

## 7. References

Dyllick, T., & Hockerts, K. (2002). Beyond the business case for corporate sustainability. *Business Strategy and the Environment*, 11(2), 130-141.

Elkington, J. (1997). *Cannibals with forks: The triple bottom line of the 21st-century business.* Oxford: Capstone Publishing.

Felber, C. (2010). *Die Gemeinwohl-Ökonomie Das Wirtschaftsmodell der Zukunft.* München: Verlag Deuticke *(Heute* Carl Hanser Verlag).

Felber, C. (2015). *Change Everything: Creating an Economy for the Common Good.* Vienna: Zen Books.

Felber, C. (2019). *This Is Not Economy.* Carl Hanser Verlag, München.

Freeman, R.E (1984). *Strategic Management: A stakeholder Approach.* Boston, MA: Pitman.

Giesenbauer, B. & Müller-Christ, C. (2018). *Die Sustainable Development Goals für und durch KMU – Ein Leitfaden für kleine und mittlere Unternehmen.* Bremen: RennNord.

Johnson, M. P. & Schaltegger, S. (2016). "Two decades of sustainability management tools for SMEs: how far have we come?". *Journal of Small Business Management*, 54(2), 481-505.

Joyce, A., & Paquin, R. L. (2016). "The triple layered business model canvas: A tool to design more sustainable business models". *Journal of Cleaner Production*, 135, 1474-1486.

Meynhardt, T. & Fröhlich, A. (2017). „Die Gemeinwohl-Bilanz – Wichtige Anstöße, aber im Legitimationsdefizit". https://www.researchgate.net/publication/320521448_Die_Gemeinwohl-Bilanz_-_Wichtige_Anstosse_aber_im_Legitimationsdefizit DOI 10.5771/0344-9777-2017-2-3-152

Porter, M.E. & Kramer, M.R. (2006). Strategy and society: The link between competitive advantage and corporate social responsibility. *Harvard Business Review*, 84(12), S. 78—92.

Schulmeister, S. (2014). *Die „Gemeinwohlökonomie" - ein wissenschaftliches Konzept und (daher) ein geeigneter Gegenstand eines Universitätslehrgangs?* Stellungnahme auf Ersuchen der Universität Salzburg, Mai2014. https://stephanschulmeister.wifo-pens.at/fileadmin/homepage_schulmeister/files/GWO__Uni_Salzburg_04_14.pdf

# "Mental sustainability": four process models – Introducing new patterns of language and thought for a sustainable world

(enriched with an anecdote from the movement of the Economy for the Common Good)

*Bernd Fittkau (with completions from) Günter Koch*

To begin with: "Problems can never be solved in the same way of thinking that created them" (Einstein).

Following this advice, we will try to do our best to identify one "alternative" way of acquiring an understanding, how a new economic "philosophy" can be adopted.
This his discussion is structured in the following six aspects in an overview:

(0) Instead of an introduction: Homage to Bernd Fittkau (by Günter Koch)

(1) Preliminary considerations and basis of the discourse

(2) The great challenges of the 21st century (Harari)

(3) People need orientation

(4) Social neo-liberal system offer: orientation towards "money

(5) Cultural alternative: Orientation towards values (ethics)

(6) Orientation towards four sustainable mental sustainability models

(7) References

## 0. Instead of an introduction: An homage to Bernd Fittkau (by Günter Koch)

Bernd Fittkau has given a, if not the keynote of the ECGPW 2019 conference and has authored a contribution to it, which would have gone far beyond the scope and length of the present conference volume. The original agreement between Bernd and me was that I would provide the English version and in that honor I would act as co-author. But that seemed to be too much of an appreciation and so I declare myself to be a companion in this contribution, which Bernd, on the advice of Tim Goydke and myself, had to streamline considerably.

I do not know whether I do justice to its original author with my editing of the chapter now presented. However, it is of great concern to me to praise Bernd Fittkau, who will soon be completing his eighth decade of life (while I have just begun it), as a thought leader and in his role as a champion for the cause of the Economy for the Common Good. Bernd is presented in Wikipedia as follows: He is a German humanistic psychologist who, together with a colleague, developed and implemented communication training for managers from 1970 onwards. After his habilitation, he served as Professor of Educational Psychology and Counselling at the University of Göttingen from 1973 to 2005. He received further training in various consulting-relevant procedures of humanistic psychology such as client-centred conversational therapy, Gestalttherapy and hypnotherapy.

The main focus of his scientific work, even after his retirement, was and still is communication psychology, methods of communication training, resource-activating consulting methods, executive coaching, team development, process-oriented project management, value management, balance in the third phase of life. From this in particular:

- the development of tests for the assessment of superior behaviour by employees
- the development of a "fear questionnaire" for pupils
- Participation in the scientific advisory board for the German issue of the pre-school TV programme "Sesamstraße"
- Development and implementation of a curriculum for "pedagogical counselling" in cooperation with colleagues, including the creation of a corresponding main study focus on a Master's programme.

In other words: Bernd Fittkau is a hero in the subject of mental mastery of educational and communication processes and with this competence he has designed his lecture for the participants of our 2019 "Gemeinwohl-Konferenz" (ECGPW-2019, which is the conference reported here) and received a great response from the audience: After all, he struck a chord that was at least as important to the majority of participants as the purely professional elaboration of the central question of this conference, namely whether and how the public welfare economy, the Economy for the Common Good, and the movement supporting it can demonstrate scientific foundations. The fascination Bernd exerted on the auditorium (and on me in the follow-up discussion) can only be hinted at in words in the following sections. All the more important are the interspersed, explanatory pictures, which Bernd's talk was accompanied by in the form of a PPT sequence and which for technical reasons could only be partially translated into English and presented here. (I am confident, however, that German terminology can be interpreted from the context).

When the final version of this paper was compiled, Wolf Lotter in August 2020 in a preliminary essay in the Austrian newspaper DER STANDARD published an article entitled "Kontext macht klug" (Context makes you smart), which addresses the question of "proper" knowledge management and argues very convincingly that it is the understanding of contexts and not the operational implementation of knowledge that enables new insights and forward developments. Bernd Fittkau has made exactly this attempt: Not only to understand in a narrow sense how mental constitution interacts with the willingness to engage in the cause of the economy for the common good, but also to understand that a future economic system must demonstrate the power to represent the diversity of social needs in their contexts.

## 1. Preliminary considerations and basis of the discourse

The inspiration for the topic "mental sustainability" comes from the social scientist, FUTURZWEI founder and GWÖ sympathizer Harald Welzer: In the mental space "between need and satisfaction Sigmund Freud saw ... the **cradle of culture**. For it is only the **ability to replenish instincts** that has so far distinguished the human form of life from all others and produced the fantastic diversity of cultural expressions and forms ...". (Welzer 2019). A **selection of criteria of "mental sustainability"** for a cultural development could be...

-   interdisciplinary language and thought patterns that are oriented towards the holistic

-   Stimulating open-ended process perspectives for regional and global spaces

-   Activation of positive emotionality, expansion of personal resonance fields

-   ethically based, life sustaining, culturally embedded and strengthening

-   ...

## 2. The great challenges of the 21st century

The Israeli historian and world bestselling author Y. N. Harari (2019) has pointed to three major current challenges facing humanity: "We do not know what the future will be like, but we do know the three major problems: **Nuclear war, climate change, digital disruption**". He puts the latter in concrete terms: Digitisation "...will make many people economically irrelevant and thus politically powerless. People will not like that at all and for very good reasons".

## 3. People need orientation

One of the salutary basic human needs (besides belonging, self-esteem and pleasure) seems to be "orientation and control" (Grawe 2000). Values are an important and culturally unifying possibility of social orientation for people.

## 4. A social neoliberal system offert: Orientation towards money

This human desire for order and overview naturally also tempts people to accept simple offers of orientation from business and politics. **Money** is one such offer, which gains its great attraction as a means of existential security and power: "Money makes the world go round". If money is seen as a **"means" for control** (and not as a life "end"), money can be considered as cultural progress compared to the archaic control by violence (as the "right of the strongest"). Otherwise it becomes a **"dance around the golden calf"** of "Homo economicus". - In our experience, the Economy for the Common Good (German: Gemeinwohlökonomie (GWÖ)) has the potential to redirect the dominant financial-dominated economic system (with its named self-destructive side effects) in a sustainable way (see Felber 2012; 2019).

## 5. Cultural alternative: Orientation towards values (-> ethics)

"Values" are cultural orientation concepts that have grown up historically in a geopolitical space and are intended to bring people with their different characters and interests together and to give them a common way of thinking, feeling and behaviour - in versions of **ideals, goals, role models, narratives**. For a social regulatory framework, binding **(mandatory) standards = laws** are derived from such philosophy.

In our enlightened constitutions (e.g. the Basic Law of the Federal Republic of Germany("Grundgesetz")) this canon of values is formulated in a justiciable way. These are as well the guidelines and guiding ideas of our commonly committed European social and cultural system. "Money" can be used as a means of securing our existence and as an extrinsic motivator and can be used to promote these values (e.g. through tax laws). This is, amongst many more things, one aspect in what the Common Good Economy proposes.

## 6. Orientation towards mental sustainability models

Values are mental concepts of sustainability, which we have condensed into four proven (mental) sustainability models. These will be introduced and briefly explained in the following series, for reasons of shortness in pictographic format.

**(6) ad 1: Mental sustainability model (1):**
**From growth dynamics to "balance**

## Mental sustainability model (1):
### • _From the dynamics of increase to "balance"_
#### → _The mentalisation process to be aimed at :_

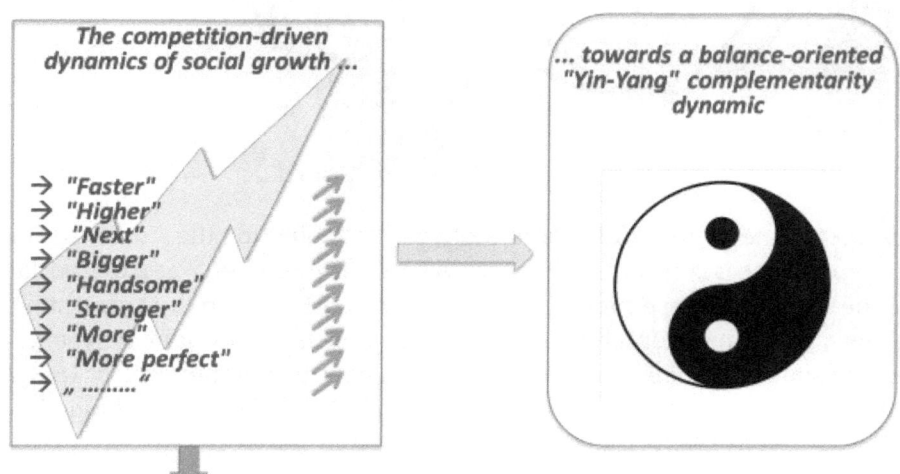

The competition-driven dynamics of social growth ...

→ _"Faster"_
→ _"Higher"_
→ _"Next"_
→ _"Bigger"_
→ _"Handsome"_
→ _"Stronger"_
→ _"More"_
→ _"More perfect"_
→ _" ........."_

... towards a balance-oriented "Yin-Yang" complementarity dynamic

Stress, BurnOut, Doping, ...
Resource-Exploitation & -Overload

→ **The GWÖ history related to this model could documented be: 50 years "Club of Rome**
From the first Club of Rome report **"The Limits to Growth"** (Meadows et al. 1972) to the last **"We're on it" ("Wir sind dran"** , Weizsäcker et al. 2018), some 50 years have passed with drastic changes:

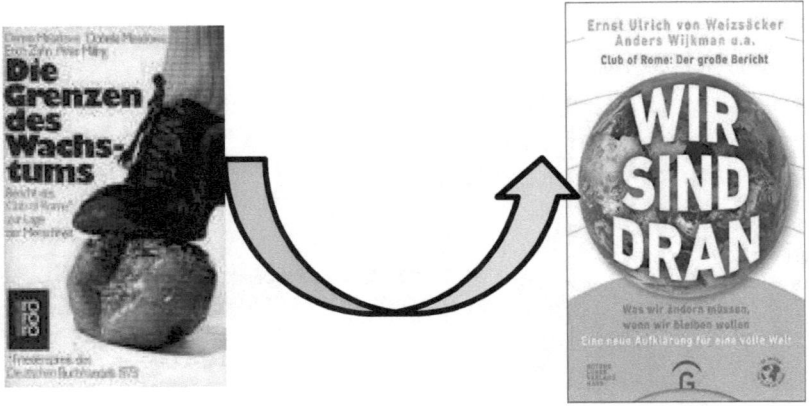

E.U. v. Weizsäcker, one of the Ambassadors of the "Economy for the Common Good" (ECG, in German: GWÖ), is currently calling for: "A new enlightenment for a full world". In this volume the ancient Chinese symbol of Yin-Yang (p. 183) becomes a central stimulus for a new thinking: "Complementarity and balance as well as the wisdom of synergy between opposites should be milestones on the way to a new enlightenment" (p. 186). And GWÖ with its basic ideas in the "Conclusions" takes on a kind of role model function (p. 378 ff).

**(6) ad 2: Mental sustainability model (2):**
**From a need- to a value-orientation**

# Mental sustainability model (2):
## • „ *From need orientation to value orientation*"

→ *The mentalisation process to be aimed at :*

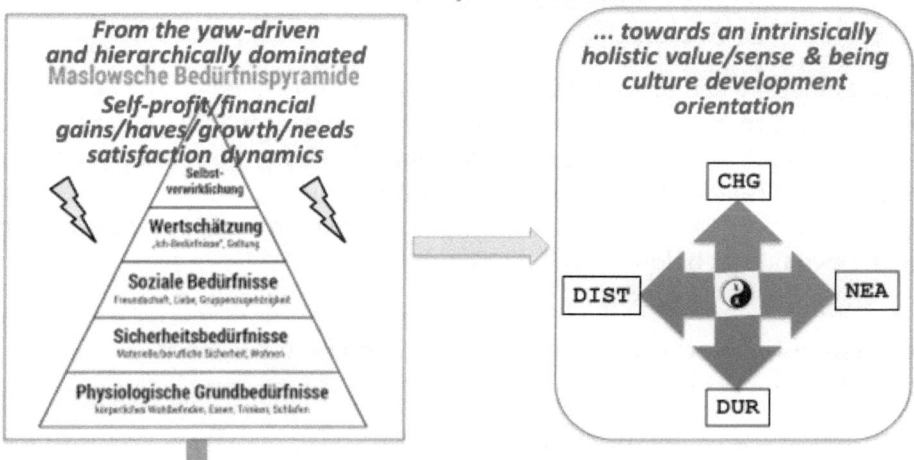

Many people know the "Pyramid of Needs" as a model for classifying human needs by the humanistic psychologist Abraham Maslow, who has set himself a monument with it. He already critically pointed out that after satisfying one level of need, the human being develops more and more needs that point beyond it. His colleague Erich Fromm took a step towards a value orientation by distinguishing between "having" and "being" needs. Maslow himself later added a value-oriented category of needs, the "transpersonal needs".

Our economic system takes advantage of our openness to needs by creatively creating new needs in marketing. The well-known Swiss economist Mathias Binswanger (2019): "We no longer live in an economy of satisfying needs, but in an economy of awakening needs. ...The system only works if we keep growing - whether we want to or not".  Man seems to be programmable to insatiability. Thus **needs themselves become a destructive growth driver**. On the "Challenges for the 21st century" outlined above (Harari 2019) it is not difficult to classify needs as "problem drivers":

## Challenges for the 21st century needs as problem drivers

| Challenges for the 21st century | Needs as problem drivers |
|---|---|
| • Tackling the ecological crises | < Growth, profit, consumption needs |
| • Prevention of nuclear wars | < Power, victory, superiority conditions |
| • Coping w. consequences of digitisation | < Omnipotence, homo deus needs |
| • Control of population growth | < Sex, desire for children, attachment |

If you may, you can easily find lists of 100s of needs. In order to classify them according to value and to manage them in a personal and socially sustainable way, we need a framework of values. The multidimensional "social space-time continuum" is a suitable balance model for this purpose (see Riemann 1969; Schulz von Thun 1989). The values of the European Enlightenment and those of the common-wealth economy can be easily categorised in it, as the two figures below show.

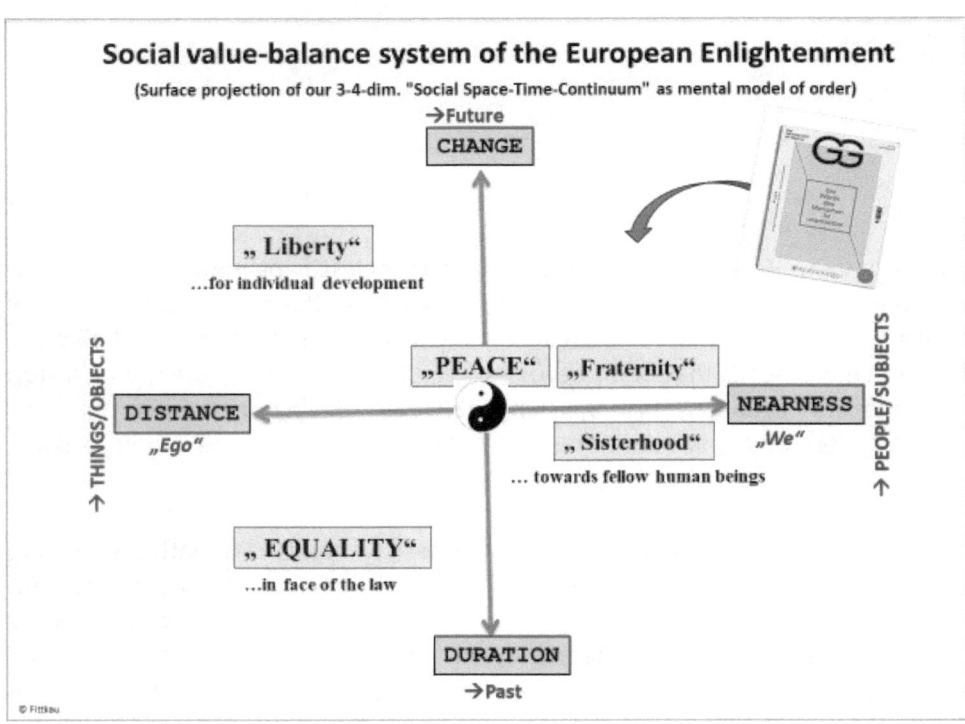

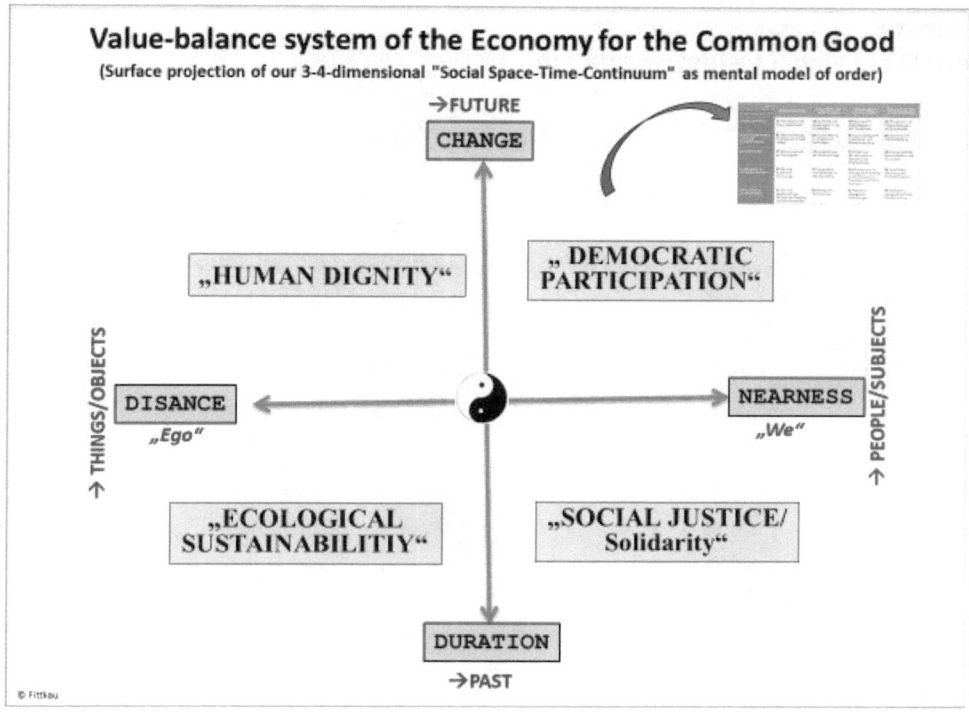

**Value-balance system of the Economy for the Common Good**

(Surface projection of our 3-4-dimensional "Social Space-Time-Continuum" as mental model of order)

By realising the canon of values of the Economy for the Common Good, the **17 globally binding sustainability goals and values (SDGs)** set out in Agenda 2030 will be promoted to a high degree (Kasper, Hofielen 2019). If these values are to be prioritised in a practice-oriented way, we need a holistic and realistic (sustainability) model.

**(6) ad 3: Mental sustainability model (3):**
**From specialist to global system orientation**

## Mental Sustainabilitiy Model (3):
### • „From specialists' orientation towards global system orientation"
### → The mentalisation process to be aimed at :

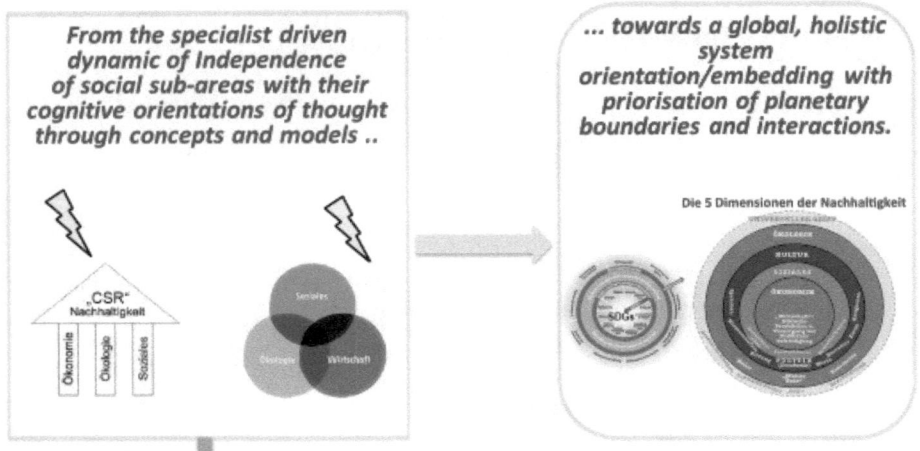

From the specialist driven
dynamic of Independence
of social sub-areas with their
cognitive orientations of thought
through concepts and models ..

... towards a global, holistic
system
orientation/embedding with
priorisation of planetary
boundaries and interactions.

"Lazy" compromises that can be fatal
between the specialist experts
without an eye for the whole

The cultural development of mankind has led to an increasing specialisation and expert focus with corresponding problematic model formations. One example is the common Corporate Social Responsibility (CSR) model of sustainability, in which only the economic, social and ecological factors are juxtaposed - and the political, cultural and spiritual factors are missing. And it is overlooked that in reality the ecological framework determines the social and the economic. The current ecological crises make this model error painfully clear to us. The above circle-subset model, supplemented by the "donut" model of ECG ambassador Kate Raworth (2018), are much more adequate model formations.

**(6) ad 4: Mental sustainability model (4):**
From the ego-centred "bread-and-games" consumption strategy to the eco-system economy

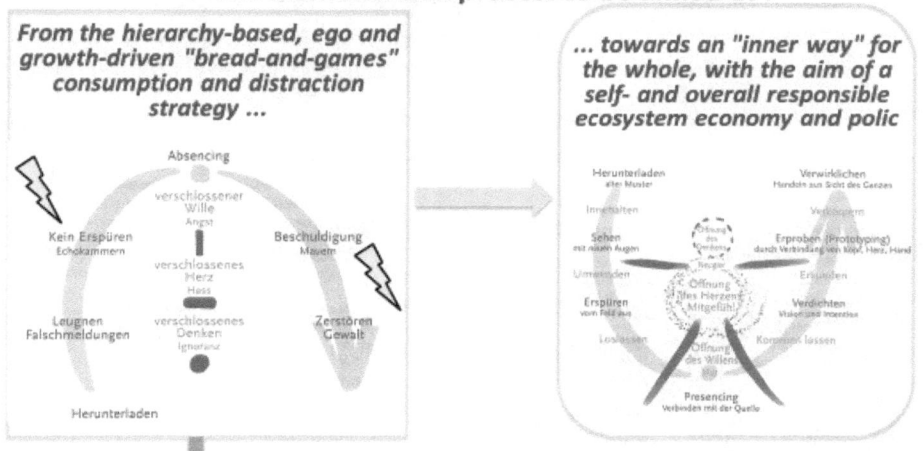

## Mental sustainability model (4):
- *„ From the ego-centred "bread and games" consumption strategy to ecosystem economy and policy"*
*(after Scharmer's „Theory U" (2019))*

→ *The mentalisation process to be aimed at :*

*From the hierarchy-based, ego and growth-driven "bread-and-games" consumption and distraction strategy ...*

*... towards an "inner way" for the whole, with the aim of a self- and overall responsible ecosystem economy and polic*

*Strengthening competition-driven ego potentials of the human being (e.g. greed-hate delusion)*

Otto Scharmer, another Ambassador of the Economy for the Common Good, developed his "Theory U" during his professional career of 25 years at MIT in Boston in a collegial circle. It is in demand worldwide as an organisational development theory and practice in politics and business. His new book "Essentials ..." (2019) provides a very readable and very personal introduction. His U-Lab-MOOC enables interested parties to gain "methods of consciousness based system change" and personal "presencing" experiences in an online course offered worldwide.

**To end: A small final conclusion on a smallish discourse as outlined above**
- **"Moral progress":** Without universal patterns of orientation and standards, nei-ther politicians nor citizens with their (alternative) movements, represented by the various NGOs, will be able to overcome our crises in a sustainable manner. Universal values are such sources of orientation. Crises have repeatedly given

humanity the opportunity to realise great "moral progress" together. In his current book "Moral Progress in Dark Times" (2020), the modern ethics scientist Markus Gabriel explains such path of cultural development.

- **"The Middle Way":** The four value orientations for a new Enlightenment discussed in this article are sufficiently clear. They focus on different universal-human potentials: the evolutionary, psychological, systemic and spiritual dimension. In doing so, the value orientations of the "Economy for the Common Good" are strengthened in an as holistic sense as possible. It is always a matter of new dynamic balances. They lead us back not the least to Aristotle, who suggested to his son Nicomachus a corresponding "middle way", documented in his Nicomachian Ethics for a Good Life (see Nicomachian Ethics - Wikipedia).

**In practice: How the suggested continuous development may be organised, especially in the context of the Economy for the Common Good, by its supporters**

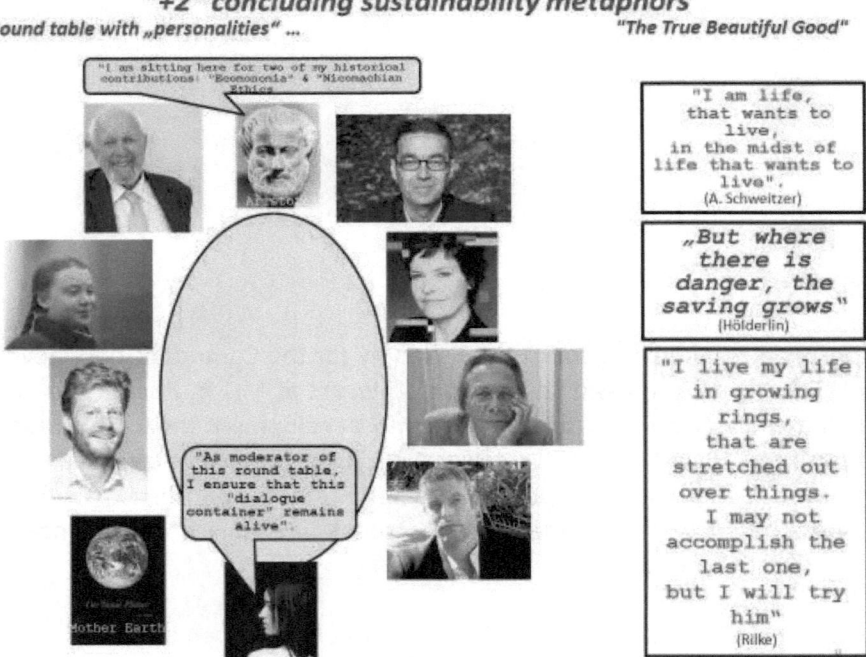

**Because it matters: An anecdotical addendum characterising the status and positioning struggle of the movement of the "Economy for the Common Good":**

**How did Christian Felber get into an Austrian textbook, criticized by academic economist?**

After Kuhn's "Structure of scientific revolutions" (see Felber 2019), the attempt of Austrian mainstream economists to mobilize Christian Felber out of a school textbook was predictable. But how did he get into it at all? To conclude, the following short story tells what may have happened in this (or perhaps in a similar way):

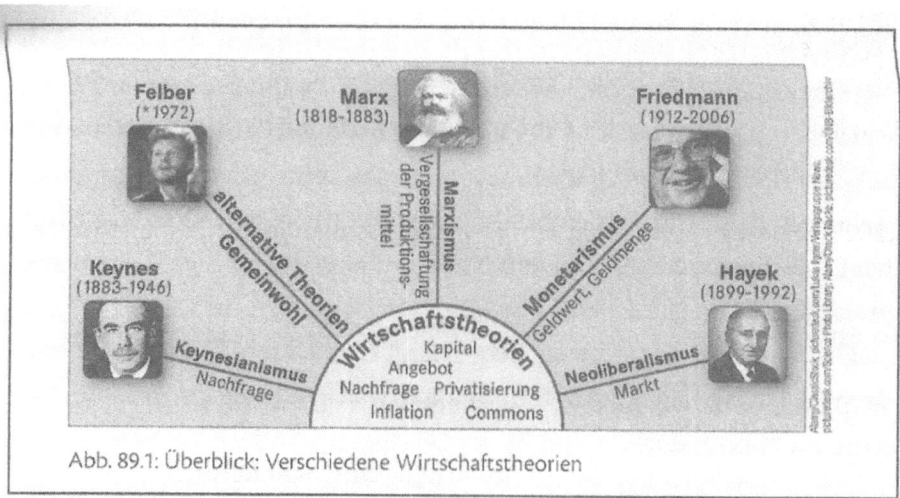

Abb. 89.1: Überblick: Verschiedene Wirtschaftstheorien

The story associated with: "The former "Minister of Education" had invited Otto Scharmer to a "U-Theory Lab" and participated in it herself. In the U-Lab process phase of concrete future project planning, she envisioned Christian Felber's presence to serve as an "alternative economic theorist" to be placed in a textbook (alongside Marx and Keynes) – and conclusively made it implemented". - A courageous politician, such kind of a person we miss so much today!

## 7. References (mostly in German)

Binswanger, M. (2019): Interview in brandeins, 09/19, S. 46-52.

Das Grundgesetz als Magazin (GG, 2019): dasgrundgesetz.de.

Felber. C. (2012): Gemeinwohl-Ökonomie –  Eine demokratische Alternative wächst. Wien: Deuticke und www.ecogood.org

Felber, C. (2019): This is not Economy – Aufruf zur Revolution der Wirtschaftswissenschaft. Wien: Deuticke.

Gabriel, M. (2020): Moralischer Fortschritt in dunklen Zeiten. Universelle Werte für das 21. Jahrhundert. Berlin. Ullstein.

Grawe, K. (2004): Neuropsychotherapie. Göttingen: Hogrefe.

Harari, Y. N. (2019): Es geht darum, den Menschen zu hacken. Interview in tazFUTURZWEI-Magazin Nr. 7, S.11ff.

Kasper, M., Hofielen, G. (2019): Punkten für das Gemeinwohl und die SDGs. Berlin: Humanistic Management Practices.

Lotter, Wolf (2020): Kontext macht klug. Vorab-Essay aus dem in der Edition Körber erschienen Buch im österreichischen STANDARD.

Nikomachische Ethik – Wikipedia: https://de.wikipedia.org/wiki/Nikomachische_Ethik

Raworth, K. (2018): Die Donut-Ökonomie. München: Blessing.

Riemann, F. (1969): Grundformen der Angst. München: Ernst-Reinhardt.

Scharmer, C. O. (2019): Essentials der Theorie U. Heidelberg: Carl-Auer.

Schulz von Thun, F. (1989): Miteinander reden 2 – Stile, Werte und Persönlichkeitsentwicklung. Reinbek: Rowohlt.

Welzer, H. (2019): Künstliche Dummheit. In taz/futurzwei, 7/2019, S. 3-10.

# The Sustainability Zeroline – a severe standard for a truly sustainable, a Regenerative Economy

*J. Daniel Dahm*

*Sustainability in the sense of future viability combines stabilization, development, protection and integrity of our common basic livelihoods and the living diversity of evolution alongside humans.*

Humans are beings in planetary connectedness, embedded in the diversity of the Earth's habitats and united in their diversity of cultures and ways of thinking from around 1.4 million years of human (co-)evolution [Lumsden, Wilson, 1981; Dahm, 2019]. Humans and the planet are moving perceptibly, almost intimately, closer together, since global circularity and ecological limitation have become part of our experience of the world. The development and expansion of their consciousness enabled humans more and more to interpret themselves in their natural habitats, to create a variety of social relationships and cooperations, and - in response to the plurality of their living realities - to unfold a multitude of cultivations of their experiences and interpretations of the world they inhabit. This interdependence between nature and culture is also the relationship between thinking and touching, between spirituality and physicality, between the tangible, physically describable reality and a fuzzy world; it confronts us with the question of ourselves and our meaning in our universe.

Between human fantasy and planetary limitations, especially in the 20th century, a blatant imbalance arose in the interplay between the anthroposphere and biogeosphere, with the result that all areas and spaces of life were transformed. »Anthropogenic greenhouse gas emissions have increased since the pre-industrial era, driven largely by economic and population growth, and are now higher than ever. This has led to atmospheric concentrations of carbon dioxide, methane and nitrous oxide that are unprecedented in at least the last 800,000 years. Their effects, together with those of other anthropogenic drivers, have been detected throughout the climate system and are extremely likely to have been the dominant cause of the observed warming since the mid-20th century.« [Intergovernmental Panel on Climate Change, 2014b]. The biogeoecological resources were consumed and depleted more and more and their regenerative capacity was in part irreversibly exceeded. Together with excessive emissions of toxins, waste and gases into landscapes, waters and the atmosphere, this led to the climatic, bio-ecological and humanitarian crisis we are facing today.

The ecological crisis becomes particularly vivid when we look at the Planetary Boundaries (= load limits of the planet) [Rockström, 2009]. These nine essential ecological dimensions for the Earth system describe and define their global limits. In 2015, the Stockholm Resilience Center announced that humanity has now left the safe zone in four dimensions: 1. climate change; 2. biodiversity; 3. land use; and 4. global phosphorus and nitrogen cycles [Steffen, 2015]. The resulting damage to the foundations of life is manifested, for example, in the increase in climate-ecological crisis scenarios due to extreme weather events and the polar collapse, but also in the loss of soils and forests and the weakening of food chains.

Since the Rio Conference in 1992, known as the "World Summit" (within the framework of the "UN Conference on Environment and Development UNCED", in which 178 states participated, the Rio Declaration, the Climate Change Convention, the Biodiversity Convention, the Forest Declaration, the Convention to Combat Desertification and Agenda 21 were adopted), which marked the beginning of a series of international follow-up conferences (Conference of Parties COP), civil society and politics have initiated many things. Never before has there been such a broad consensus that the common foundations of humanity's existence require appreciation and protection. Also the understanding that in a limited planetary sphere (ancient Greek: σφαῖρα sphaira = shell, ball) everyone depends on each other and we cannot look at ourselves in isolation from the many others has never been so pronounced in modern times. In fact, a global consciousness has found its way into people's everyday thinking, and the media reflection of this cross-border ecological interdependence also reflects this. Even though economic conflicts, nationalisms, and ethnic, religious, and social divides dominate the news, and the consumer society is globalizing in a turmoil, doubts about this progress have rarely been so evident.

At the same time, we learn that the speed with which the transformation to a sustainable society and economy is proceeding is not high enough. Even faster than we are changing ourselves, we are confronted with climatic and ecological changes that can for the most part only be understood in their basic principles [Intergovernmental Panel on Climate Change (IPCC), 2014a]. At the same time, we are experiencing a dramatic poor-rich divide with international migrations on a historically unprecedented scale. For more and more people around the globe, the first quarter of the 21st century marks an imminent turn of an era. The standards of social and economic success that were socially conveyed and learned, which many blindly followed, promised a good life through diligence, work and assertiveness, but also through the accumulation of money and goods and the desire to have more. Such traditional and learned beliefs can now only be maintained by disregarding the reality of life. The limits of consumerist lifestyles, the resilience of democratic societies and natural habitats are clearly evident. The (side) effects of material- and energy-intensive models of prosperity and their economic realization are too obvious and drastic [UNEP Finance Initiative, 2011]. Whether it is the destruction of the earth's ecological and climatic integrity or the social, cultural and political consequences of this catastrophic modernity - the triggering processes and drivers of the consumption of resources and ecological substance and the pollution and destruction of nature are well known and undeniable.

The economic practice of the last decades perverted the enlightening idea of economy and markets and turned it upside down. What was supposed to create prosperity, freedom, justice and peace resulted in a sweeping attack against all living things. Sustainability in the sense of future viability became the most important paradigm of human development in the face of measurable changes in the planetary ecosystem. Decisive for a turnaround and the future development of mankind and its institutions is the focus and function of economic activities and their implementation, especially in entrepreneurial activities.

Sustainability in economic activity presupposes that economic activities and investment capital have the effect of strengthening the common goods of the biogeosphere and the anthroposphere. If sustainable development is a core condition for successful economic practice, then one of the core tasks of markets is to enable, secure and drive the sustainability or vitality of life. One is clear: if sustainability serves life, it requires more than the preservation of substance. Only with the (re)construction of the degraded life systems and the renaturation and recultivation of the damaged biocapacity of the planet does real sustainability begin. [...] The most important achievement that humanity has to accomplish is to balance the debt to the planetary common goods so that we can write an ecological "black zero" - a sustainability zero.

Sustainability in the sense of future viability is the goal and measure by which humanity must measure all its activities, above all economic activities. If sustainability is taken as a normative criterion for success and thus as a minimum condition for economic success, the progressive externalization of negative effects is categorically ruled out, or rather it discredits economic success and turns it into its opposite.

Economics should [accordingly] be life-serving, i.e. it should serve the evolutionary capacity of the vitality of ecosystems and their diversity and resilience, including humans. If sustainability is not increased, there can be no question of economic success.

Based on a strict definition for sustainability and future viability, the sustainability zero-point, is drawn to a sustainability zero line, the Sustainability Zeroline Benchmark [Dahm, 2019].

The Sustainability Zeroline is an artificial concept that resulted from a long examination of externalization processes, their causes and effects and a spontaneous idea. Externalizations of damage, usually from private sector processes into the commons [Dahm, 2013], form a counter-process to sustainability [Dahm, 2015; Dahm, 2019]. This is symbolized, among other things, by the presentation of the global overshoot [Global Footprint Network, 2010] and the life-destroying implications resulting from it. Humankind damages the future if it consumes more of its natural resources than can be regenerated through natural value creation [Scherhorn, 2010]. If this is continued over a longer period of time, it gradually robs us of our natural resources [Weizsäcker, 1989].

So, if the definition of sustainability used so far also deals with the preservation of the natural and cultural bases of life, it follows that these must not be damaged or reduced to a minimum. This is the absolute minimum that results as a measure of sustainable development: the exclusion of the continued depletion and damage to our planetary bases of life - the exclusion of negative effects.

The Sustainability Zeroline is an impact-oriented benchmark and measures the effectiveness of economic activity on the commons of the biogeosphere and anthroposphere:

I. Sustainability begins at a zero line along which the full integrity of the biogeosphere, including humans, is maintained.

II. If the sum of (1) externalization of negative effects, (2) internalization, (3) compensation/compensation measures and (4) positive effects is less than or equal to zero, then this is not a sustainable economic activity; it produces more harm than good and would be better left out.

III. As a formula, the Sustainability Zeroline is defined as follows:

IV. (internalisation + compensation + good impact) − (externalisation of negative effects) ≤ 0

V. Sustainability is not, if negative effects on biogeosphere and anthroposphere common goods arise and remain.

VI. From the Sustainability Zeroline onwards, the preservation of the natural and cultural basis of life is guaranteed. Only here sustainability begins. Sustainability is ensured by:

a. Resource-conserving and socially friendly economic methods that out-source zero ecologically, socially and culturally negative effects (damage), or compensate for them fully and completely in terms of quality and quantity.

b. Achieving the sustainability zero can initially only guarantee the preservation of the stock and this only if the stock is not already in free fall because it is already severely destabilized. This must be assumed for a large part of the planetary commons: They have already been damaged many times, ecologically degraded and desertified.

VI. Sustainability in the sense of future viability requires:

a. the gradual equalization of the ecological debt of humankind and

b. the build-up of an ecological buffer.

Sustainability not only preserves and protects the commons of the biogeosphere and anthroposphere, but also enriches, strengthens and vitalizes them. In addition to avoidance, internalization and compensation, sustainability also helps to build and enhance the planetary life potential. "Lifeserving" (= good impact) becomes the key here.

The Sustainability Zeroline defines the fictitious state of a total balance between global biocapacity and the global ecological footprint as a zero-line measure - as a minimum requirement for sustainability, but one which is obviously not achieved. It offers a clear and easy to understand model for understanding the relation or mismatch between supply and demand in the earth's ecosystem. If the full planetary capacity is equal to the total demand of mankind, this can be considered as conservation of the actual state. A restoration of the fundamentals of life is thus impossible, because the regenerative capabilities of the ecosystems are completely absorbed. But at least a resting period is achieved in relation to the progressive degradation of biocapacity, which would already be a great step forward compared to the present. If, however, human demand again exceeds the supply of the planetary ecosystem, we experience an "overshoot" of our ecological demand, which is potentially fatal for our livelihoods - an overshoot. This is still often misunderstood and perceived as "growth". The Sustainability Zeroline makes it possible to communicate this context in a way that is understandable, just like a profit and loss statement for our own future.

With the ecological crisis, a new (but familiar) ethical orientation is emerging out of the objectively measurable changes of everyday conditions and possibilities of life, which calls for a spiritual as well as a practical acknowledgement of the living nature in ourselves and around us, and chooses this as a vital point of reference. This can rightfully be described as an ethic of the living (in reference to Albert Schweitzer). "I am life that wants to live, amidst of life that wants to live." [Schweitzer, 1991].

Now what calls for a further development is the design of a rebuilding, regenerative economy that serves our material and immaterial foundations of life - the commons - driven by empathy and serving life. This is my response to the degradation and the destruction processes in the biogeosphere, which are threatening the future of all of us and robbing us the air to breathe and the space in which we can flourish.

# Bibliography

Aristoteles (2006): Nikomachische Ethik. Reinbek.

Bourdieu, Pierre (1983): Ökonomisches Kapital, kulturelles Kapital, soziales Kapital. In: Kreckel, R. [Hg.](1983): Soziale Ungleichheiten. Soziale Welt Sonderband 2, Göttingen.

Dahm, Daniel; Scherhorn, Gerhard (2008): Urbane Subsistenz. Die zweite Quelle des Wohlstands. München.

Dahm, Daniel (2009): Prinzipien einer ökologisch sozialen Marktwirtschaft. Basispapier zu einer zukunftsfähigen Wirtschaftsordnung. Berlin.

Dahm, Daniel (2013): Marktwirtschaft ohne Externalisierung oder: die Überwindung des Overshoot. Toblacher Gespräche 2013. Mit UnternehmerGeist die großen Transformationen wagen. Akademie der Toblacher Gespräche, Toblach, Südtirol, Italien.

Dahm, Daniel (2015): Corporate Sustainable Restructuring (CSR). In: Depping, A.; Walden, D. [Hg.] (2015): CSR und Recht. Juristische Aspekte nachhaltiger Unternehmensführung erkennen und verstehen. Springer. Berlin.

Dahm, Daniel (2019): Benchmark Nachhaltigkeit. Sustainability Zeroline. Maß einer zukunftsfähigen Ökonomie. Bielefeld.

Daly, Herman (2015): Economics for a Full World. London.

Dürr, Hans-Peter (2011): Das Lebende lebendiger werden lassen. München.

Global Footprint Network (2010): Ecological Footprint Atlas. www.footprintnetwork.org Intergovernmental Panel on Climate Change (IPCC) (2014a): Climate Change 2013. The physical science basis. Summary for policymakers. Working Group I.

Intergovernmental Panel on Climate Change (IPCC) (2014b): Approved Summary for Policymakers. Fifth Assessment. Climate Change 2014. Synthesis Report. New York.

Lumsden, Charles J.; Wilson, Edward Osborne (1981): Genes, Mind, and Culture. The Coevolutionary Process. Cambridge.

Papst Franziskus I. (2015): Laudato Si' – Über die Sorge für das gemeinsame Haus. http://w2.vatican.va/content/dam/francesco/pdf/encyclicals/documents/papa-francesco_20150524_enciclica-laudato-si_ge.pdf

Rockström, et al. (2009): Planetary boundaries. Exploring the safe operating space for humanity. In: Ecology and Society.

Scherhorn, Gerhard (2010): Die Politik in der Wachstumsfalle. Rehburg-Loccum: Evangelische Akademie.

Scherhorn, Gerhard (2013): Das Gegenteil von Nachhaltigkeit ist Externalisierung. Vortragsskript. Köln.

Schweitzer, Albert (1991): Die Ehrfurcht vor dem Leben – Grundtexte aus fünf Jahrzehnten. 6. Auflage. München.

Steffen, Will; Richardson, Katherine; Rockström, Johan; Gerten, Dieter; Heinke, Jens et al. (2015): Planetary Boundaries: guiding human development on a changing planet. In: Science. DOI: https://doi.org/10.1126/science.1259855

Stiglitz, Joseph; Sen, Amartya; Fitoussi, Jean-Paul (2009): Report by the Commission on the Measurement of Economic Performance and Social Progress. Paris.

UNEP Finance Initiative (2011): Universal Ownership. Why environmental externalities matter to institutional investors. www.trucost.com/_uploads/publishedResearch/Universal_Ownership_UNPRI_UNEPFI.pdf

Weizsäcker, Ernst Ulrich (1989): Erdpolitik. Wissenschaftliche Buchgesellschaft. Darm-
stadt.

# Contribution to Knowledge-based Development from the Commons Theory

*Maria Angelica Jung Marques, Jamile Sabatini Marques, Blanca C. Garcia, Tatiana Tucunduva Philippi Cortese*

## 1. Introduction

Knowledge-based development (KBD) is a scientific field, based on the social process of knowledge as endogenous value-creation. It explores a community's potential and its local resources to achieve sustainable development, and therefore has been adopted by several cities in the world as a sustainable development strategy (Carrillo, 2002, 2004; Yigitcanlar, 2010, 2011).

From several studies published in the field of KBD, one can observe its composite perspective, starting from the individual and from the organizational to the social, from the physical dimensions of proximity to social dimensions such as culture and trust, from geography to anthropology (Carrillo, Metaxiotis & Yigitcanlar, 2010). KBD is a multidisciplinary field of study that derives and uses the convergence of several disciplines, such as economics, urbanism, geography, psychology, computer science, sociology, anthropology and political science (Carrillo & Batra, 2012).

The concept of KBD came to urban planning and development during the twentieth century with the goal of supporting the transformation of cities into knowledge cities and societies into knowledge societies, which require conditions and environments distinct from those based on industrial economics (Knight, 1995). However, the redefinition of the concept has become a necessity during the first decade of the 21st century, especially in the areas of economy, society, management and technology, along with severe climate change (Yigitcanlar, 2011 p.63).

For Carrillo (2014), despite the wide use of concepts such as knowledge economy, knowledge societies and knowledge cities, there is still a need for solid KBD definitions. Even in specialized circles, the central concept of knowledge-based development has a series of interpretations (Carrillo, 2014). In this sense, the author presents three objectives for KBD: two main objectives - (i) knowledge for economic prosperity and (ii) knowledge for human development; and (iii) contributing to a sustainable society (socially and environmentally) where knowledge is the facilitator of an evolutionary future (figure

1), putting sustainability in focus and giving direction and meaning to related knowledge strategies.

*Figure 1 - The three KBD objectives (Carrillo, 2014)*

By including this third objective, the author notes that it is necessary to consider that those living in a knowledge economy are knowledge citizens, which means a better educated population (formal or informal), critical and informed - ready to participate in civic life, politically active, interested in a better quality of life for themselves and for the next generation, including concern for healthy and less dependent on consumption, appreciating artistic expression and cultural activities, and more competent in human relations (Carrillo, 2014).

Yigitcanlar et al. (2018) consider as a desired outcome in terms of an economic development in smart cities: Cities should have the capability of developing their technologies unique to solve their developmental needs. This can contribute to create a local innovation economy and prosperity that is a central element of smart cities. This outcome connects with open data as a commons that generates prosperity in a city, and creates new way of consumption and wellbeing.

Considering the objectives of the KBD and the concepts of smart cities, it was proposed by Lara et al. (2016 p. 9), that a Smart City is "A community that systematically promotes the overall wellbeing for all of its members, and flexible enough to proactively and sustainably become an increasingly better place to live, work and play".

Another perspective of Knowledge-Based Urban Development (KBUD) and Smart Cities, is the concept of Smart City 4.0 (figure 2). It is an urban locality functioning as a healthy system of systems with sustainable and balanced practices of economic, societal, environmental and governance activities generating desired outcomes for all humans and non-humans (Yigitcanlar et al., 2018).

*Figure 2 - KBUD - Framework proposed by Yigitcanlar et al. (2018)*

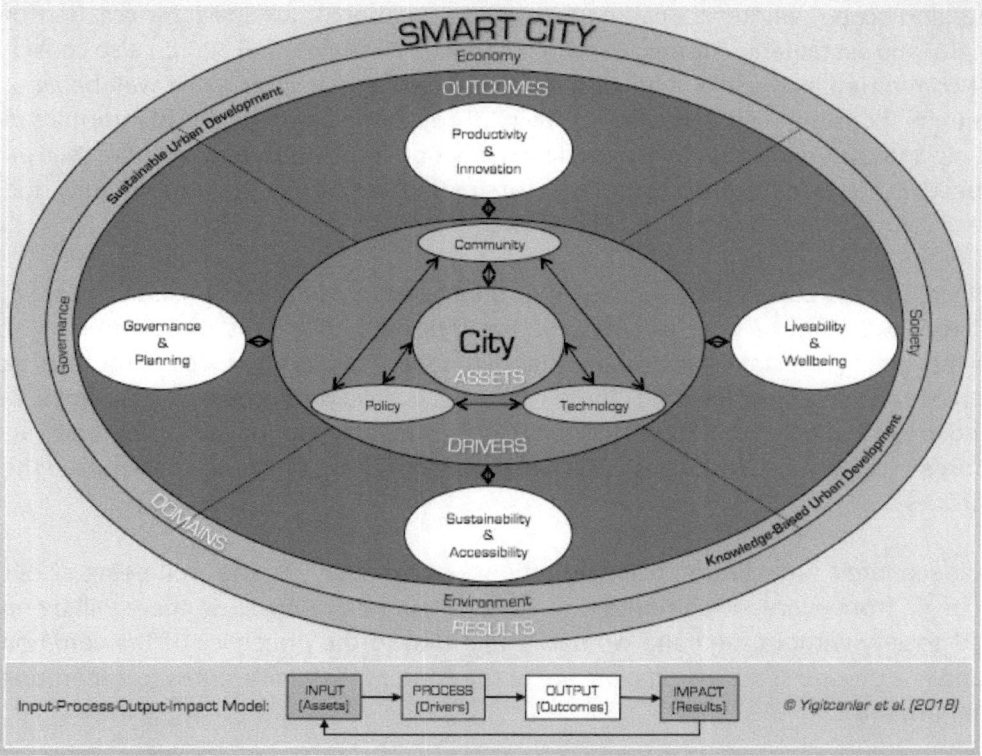

A city that has the assets as inputs, the community, policy and technology as part of the process and drivers in order generate as an output (i) economy domain: productivity & innovation, (ii) environment domain: sustainability & accessibility; (iii) governance domain: governance & planning and (iv) Society domain: Liveability and wellbeing as outcomes to be considered a result a smart cities, causing impact for the society. It is important that the four domains should balance and work together for a city to be smart.

Errichiello & Marasco (2014), brings to discussion the importance of open service innovation in smart cities with a framework for exploring innovation networks in the development of new city services. Open data is a way to develop and create knowledge-based development.

Sustainability requires collaboration between governments, business and civil society at all levels and scope, whether local, national or international, for the joint creation of meaningful and sustainable futures. Carrillo (as cited in Gonzalez et al., 2005) also considers that committed leadership is fundamental to achieving the sustainable well-being of a community. Considering the interconnectivity, through the technologies of information processing and communication, transcending the geopolitical limits, and the perennial interconnectivity derived from the fact that we are members of a planetary community, the necessary commitment to successful KBD initiatives.

It is reflected in the sustainable well-being of the planetary community (Laszlo & Laszlo, 2007). From the point of view of cities, we are dealing with groups of people making choices (beginning by establishing themselves in the same territory) as well as the sharing between people (largely intangible). These two aspects have profound economic implications and are at the heart of KBD (Carrillo, 2015). This means that individuals in their various groups in society are the subject of social transformations, or agents of change in the social process.

The socioeconomic and cultural transformations so necessary for the well being of our society begin from everyone committed to the cause of justice, because there will be no renewed society without men and women committed to the principles of the common good, and it is the social process knowledge of the context that contributes to generating this commitment.

Considering that commons theory is based on principles that contribute to and support the social process, which refers to a form of community management or governance applied to a resource, and involves a group or community of people share access to use of the resource. Hence, the purpose of this paper is to answer the question: How does commons theory contribute to the field of KBD, establishing the main points of convergence between the elements of knowledge-based development and commons theory?

## 2. Methodology

The three KBD objectives, as already mentioned: (i) knowledge for economic prosperity; (ii) knowledge for human development, and (iii) the contribution to a sustainable society (socially and environmentally) and where knowledge is the facilitator of an evolutionary future or futures, bring with it some basic assumptions. These assumptions include the need to develop collective planning and management actions for development, using the knowledge to do so; solving complex and interdisciplinary problems; and the need to manage conflicts and interests of various parts of society.

From these assumptions, an analysis was made of the similarities and differences between the KBD theory and the Commons theory, looking for the existing literature on both, as well as other empirical studies that could bring different lenses to aid in the analysis. In the analysis of the commons theory, the literature on knowledge commons and urban commons was searched for its closest focus with the challenges of city development, and for a limitation of the scope of this study.

Analysing recent articles of relevance, published in journals of high impact, one notices the lack of connection between the commons and smart cities and also on knowledge-based development, bringing a relevance to research on the subject. In the article entitled "Can cities become smart without being sustainable? A systematic review of the literature", published at Sustainable Cities and Society by Yigitcanlar et al, (2018), come up with only one article about commons. The article "Introducing a taxonomy of the "smart city": towards a commons-oriented approach?" shows the importance of the commons-oriented smart city that can provide the capacity for open participation and democratic problem-solving procedures. The society engagement in the decision-making processes is essential to create a direct link between technology and the needs of city-dwellers (Niaros, 2016).

The other article "Understanding 'smart cities': Intertwining development drivers with desired outcomes in a multidimensional framework", published at Cities Journal by Yigitcanlar et al (2018), does not mention commons connected to smart cities. This article is an important one that brings the literature reviews of smart cities in the aspects of smart city frameworks, smart city and community, smart city and technology and smart city and policy.

There is a limitation in the literature that connects the themes of knowledge-based development and smart cities with commons theory. The article outline to look at the commons in the area of urban knowledge. After the comparative analyses, a discussion of the findings and recommendations for other studies is made at the discussion and conclusion section.

## 3. The Common Good Theory and the Tragedy of the Commons

Elinor Ostrom, a Nobel laureate in economics in 2009, began exploring common pool resource management in the 1970s as an extension of her dissertation and subsequent research on institutional arrangements for public water management in Southern California. Her publication in 1977, co-authored with her husband, Vincent Ostrom, "A Theory for Institutional Analysis of Common Pool Resources" argued that the articulation of institutions is the critical factor in effective management of common resources.

Throughout the 1980s, from a large volume of empirical research, Ostrom highlighted successful international case studies of successfully managed commons, which were then analysed to allow the identification of shared governance characteristics that seemed to form generalizable principles (Kaunekis, 2014). The results inspired the eight commons principles reported by Ostrom in Governing the Commons (Ostrom, 1990), from a model in which a group organizes, sets rules, applies systems, and monitors compliance. The principles established by Ostrom are a set of conditions existing in self-organized and self-governing groups with success in collective action.

The key in establishing institutions to effectively manage commons is the consideration of equity, efficiency and sustainability (Hess & Ostrom, 2007). Equity concerns fair ownership and contribution to the maintenance of the resource or common good. Efficiency refers to the optimal production, management, and use of the common good. Sustainability focuses on long-term results and is concerned with the well being of the common good users in the future.

Commoners, which Ostrom has also called appropriators, need to create rules of appropriation restricted to time, place, technology and quantity of resources that are clearly related to local conditions, as well as to create rules of supply that demand work, material, and money. In successful examples, Ostrom found that most individuals affected by operational rules could participate in modifying them, which meant that there were collective choice agreements. Ostrom concluded that monitoring the conditions of the common resource and more common behaviour is a critical function for the success of collective action as well as the need to monitor action.

Successfully managed common land studied by Ostrom generally had penalties for offenders. Such common goods had clearly defined and low-cost conflict resolution mechanisms. In addition, the rights of citizens to design their own institutions have not been challenged by government authorities in successful common goods. Overall, Ostrom concluded that effectiveness for commons management requires "successful collective action and self-governing behaviour; trust and reciprocity; and the continuous design and/or evolution of appropriate rules" (Hess & Ostrom, 2007, p.43).

In 2008, Charlotte Hess elaborates on a number of questions about how people come to the commons and what motivations lead to the naming of resources as a common good in order to respond to the diverse definitions and understanding of new insights about commons (Hess, 2008). The author observes, in the review of works on new common goods meanings and uses different from the "Commons" as a descriptor of a resource, movement or phenomenon, however, realizes that all have a sense of sharing and joint ownership as: (i) the need to protect a shared resource of enclosure, privatization or commodification; (ii) the observation or action of production in pairs and mass collaboration mainly in electronic media; (iii) evidence of new types of commons tragedies; (iv) the desire to build civic education and common thinking; (v) identification of new or developing types of common goods within traditional common goods; and (vi) rediscovery of the commons goods (Hess, 2008).

Examining the wide variety of new commons, Hess (2008, p.39) makes a set of observations:

- Collaboration and cooperation are particularly vibrant in knowledge and in the common community;

- Many new common goods are on a much larger scale, usually global; at the same time, there is an increasing sense of commons at the local level;

- Often there is a broader view of responsibility - "beyond our own backyard." It is the positive side of globalization that there is greater awareness of geographically remote communities. Even the common goods of the neighbourhood, which can be focused only on local issues, are often mindful of the impact of current decisions on future generations;

- Sustainability is a ubiquitous issue. Often there is an effective management vision for the preservation and sustainability of a resource;

- Equity is often an important consideration in new commons;

- The "Gift Economy" concept is becoming more familiar;

- Users of commons resources are often aware of their interdependence;

- Unlike public goods, commons are vulnerable to failure through invasion, privatization, commercialization, congestion, scarcity, degradation;

- Appropriate rules are needed to govern the resource.

This paper discusses the knowledge and urban commons concepts that, given their nature and breadth, may have a greater correlation with the KBD approach, but other new commons definitions can contribute as well.

## 4. Knowledge Commons

In the early 2000s, Ostrom and Hess recognized the emerging importance of knowledge commons as a research area and began applying the Institutional Analysis and Development (IAD) framework to commons analysis (Ostrom & Hess, 2007). For authors, knowledge commons refer to commons arrangements to overcome various social dilemmas associated with sharing and producing information, innovation, and creative work (Ostrom & Hess, 2006).

Madison, Frischmann, & Strandburg (2010) developed a research structure specifically adapted to the properties that distinguish knowledge and information from natural resources (Madison et al., 2010). These authors consider that human intervention constructs resources in the knowledge commons, rather than being found in some way in nature. They consider it a broad term, including cultural commons as cultural heritage, for example. Madison et al. (2010) appropriate successful methods for the natural environment to develop a systematic and detailed study of commons arrangements proposing a framework for the study of knowledge commons that initially uses the Institutional Analysis and Development (IAD) structure developed and used by Elinor Ostrom and others and adapt it to unique attributes of knowledge and information.

The framework of knowledge commons governance (Madison et al., 2010; Frischmann, Madison, & Strandburg, 2014) is based on three basic propositions: (i) the traditional "free rider" theory of intellectual property does not explain cooperative institutions to create and share knowledge that are predominant (and perhaps more and more) in society, consequently a policy based exclusively on this traditional view is incapable of promoting the creative work of social value that is best governed by a commons approach and may possibly prevent such work; (ii) the widespread recognition of certain known commons successes, such as open source software, can be problematic when it ignores the significant governance challenges that often arise for these institutions, (iii) the development of a more sophisticated approach to knowledge commons governance will require a systematic empirical study of the governance of common knowledge "in nature".

Frischmann and his colleagues (2014) make an analogy between the cultural environment and the natural environment to explore the proposition that, just as natural resources are usually governed by common goods, rather than being managed as public or private property, production and knowledge sharing is often underpinned by common governance. The book "Governing Knowledge Commons" (2014), explores how the knowledge commons work, the place they occupy in the cultural environment, the specific benefits they offer, the costs and risks they create and their relationships with other institutional structures. The authors identify knowledge commons as an independent and affirmative way to produce innovation and creativity and as an important research domain, understanding that the commons are not totally independent, nor are they opposed to markets based on exclusive (formal or informal) rights, nor are subordinated to them (Frischmann et al., 2014).

Knowledge commons cannot be physically limited; nor are they marked by the subtractability that defines the commons of natural resources. On the opposite, when one uses knowledge, one not only withdraws from ordinary knowledge; is added to it (Hess & Ostrom, 2007).

## 5. Urban Commons

The notion of urban commons refers to shared resources in the urban context; resources that are accessed and used by different participants and whose long-term sustainability depends on how these different uses come into action and interact with each other (Foster, 2011). However, there is still little empirical research that explicitly theorizes the urban commons, despite the growing interest in cities as places of social struggle, as well as the contemporary concern for urban justice (Harvey, 2008). Most commons research does not explicitly address the urban, although Ostrom (2007), and law scholars like Foster (2011), have drawn attention to the urban commons.

However, the city is a good place to test the theory of commons, because the city is an environment that brings complexities by being more densely populated; to be eminently social spaces, and therefore with more potential for conflict; and are more subject to rapid change than less populated areas. As Harvey argues, the urban commons "represents all the commons political contradictions in a highly concentrated way" (Harvey, 2012, p. 80).

Foster (2011) addresses some challenges for urban commons, noting that in traditional commons, public authorities are generally not involved in collaborative management, but when it comes to urban commons, such involvement seems inevitable. The author exemplifies how the explosion of urban agriculture has opened channels for more collaborative forms of green space management in cities, and as in this case resources are often publicly known, and management is "open" to more collaborative and inclusive forms.

Foster also highlights that there are cases where public authorities are directly involved in the commons by having public officials cooperating with citizens, NGOs and companies in managing a specific resource (e.g. business innovation district, which entails the creation of a cooperative between city, landowners and real estate developers for neighbourhood improvement), and argues that there is a need to articulate even more the role of public authorities as facilitators and participants in urban commons (Foster, 2011). However, the actors involved may have different interests, the involvement of the public sector, citizens, private sector actors and the third sector means to gather different values and preferences as to what uses the common goods can support and thus how the management (Foster, 2011), and when rational arrangements where collective interest is understood by users as a way to increase their individual long-term gain. The traditional way in which collaborative management is understood in the commons field does not allow articulation and understanding of these different values (Nightingale, 2011).

It is also important to consider the "irrational" elements of the commons, which implies observing how subjectivity is at stake in collective action, considering the different understandings that are present and how they are negotiated, as well as looking at power in the relationships between users (Nightingale, 2011). Recently Harvey (2012) theorized widely about urban commons, considering the concept promising, however, the author is concerned with elucidating how commons could "scale" and work at macro levels (Harvey, 2012).

For Harvey (2008, p.103) it is even possible to see "the metropolis as a factory for commons production". The human qualities of the city emerge from our practices in the various spaces of the city, even when these spaces are subject to enclosure by both private and public state ownership, as well as by social control, appropriation and countermeasures, to affirm what Henri Lefebvre called "the right to the city" by the inhabitants. Through their daily activities and struggles, individuals and social groups create the social world of the city and in doing so, create something common as a framework within which all of us can inhabit. Although this culturally creative common cannot be destroyed by use, it can be degraded and undervalued through excessive abuse.

To have the right to the city, as Harvey argues, is beyond the needs of individuals and their communities to have certain access to the resources of this existential medium. Law is not only a guarantee of public benefits, or fullness of salutary living conditions for all citizens, as it prospects the ideology of the democratization of urban spaces. The right to the city must also allow the right to change and reinvent the urban environment itself. In this sense, the subject of law is not only the citizen who is the beneficiary of political guarantees, but an interacting actor who must have his transforming biophysical spaces, infrastructures and politicians of the city understood, recognized and protected by the formal value of his citizenship (Harvey 2012).

## 6. The Commons Contribution to Knowledge-based Development

Cities are places of relatively intense competition for land because they have relatively high densities of the human population. A large number of people in a relatively small amount of space mean that these people are more forced to share or compete for resources. As cities are densely populated and co-created by a diversity of people, with different ideas about commons - ideas about who should manage what common goods and how - there is always a generation of conflict. Cities are places where a wide variety of people coexist, in contrast to a village or small isolated communities in which people share more in terms of values and intentions. Harvey insists commons are always contested. "A common good - he writes - may need to be protected at the expense of another" (Harvey, 2011, p.102). For example, in the Lower East Side of New York in the 1980s, community gardens were occupying lands that could be used for a different form of common goods: accessible housing (Schmelzkopf, 1995).

Finally, the city itself is the locus of the commons designed more broadly. In essence, the city is the physical manifestation of a positive balance generated collectively; cities have emerged as places to store the wealth of a society (Harvey, 2008). For Hardt and Negri, the metropolis is what generates the commons. The metropolis is where people come together and meet each other in unexpected ways, working together to create culture. The city, they write, "is the source of the common and the receptacle to which it flows" (Hardt & Negri 2009, p.154).

In a development context, knowledge flows or even "leaks" from those who have created it to a broader spectrum of society, who are the beneficiaries of KBD. In this sense, knowledge tends to become a public good, despite the existence of several linguistic, social and cognitive barriers against the diffusion of knowledge (Ferreira & Neto, 2005).

The multidisciplinary nature of KBD is complex, and some of its source disciplines are undergoing revolutionary transformations, impacting the conceptual foundations of KBD's new field, due to the dynamic nature of all scientific fields that provide continuous reinterpretations of contributing theoretical substrates (Carrillo & Batra, 2012). The authors note that the apparent subversion of the major social and economic constructs (e.g. development, democracy, government, market, price, money, business, property,...), as well as the emergence of new ones (e.g. social networks, crowdsourcing, open systems, collective intelligence, uniqueness,...) add a significant level of difficulty to the understanding and management of KBD realities, and it is increasingly apparent that the formal configuration of the field somehow depends on a perspective systemic.

At the same time, discussions about commons and their understanding and application have also evolved over time. The emphasis on the commons' social nature allows an understanding of the commons that are explicitly created by humans, including the intangible world of ideas and the built environment of cities. In this sense, some points of convergence between the elements of knowledge-based development and its evolution and commons principles can be highlighted (figure 3).

*Figure 3 – The convergence between the elements of knowledge-based development and its evolution and commons principles*

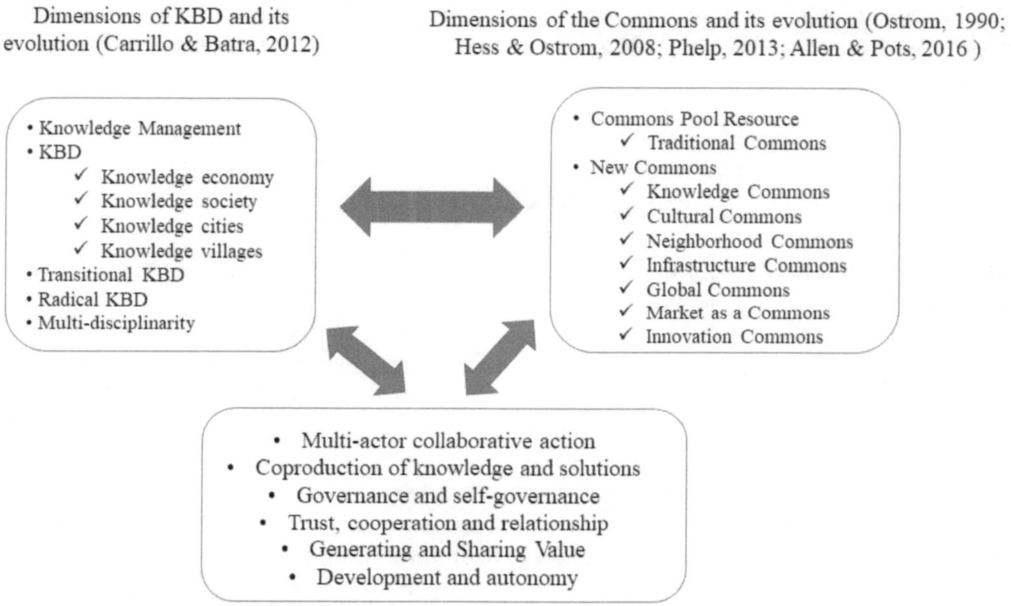

Dimensions of KBD and its evolution (Carrillo & Batra, 2012)

Dimensions of the Commons and its evolution (Ostrom, 1990; Hess & Ostrom, 2008; Phelp, 2013; Allen & Pots, 2016 )

- Knowledge Management
- KBD
  - ✓ Knowledge economy
  - ✓ Knowledge society
  - ✓ Knowledge cities
  - ✓ Knowledge villages
- Transitional KBD
- Radical KBD
- Multi-disciplinarity

- Commons Pool Resource
  - ✓ Traditional Commons
- New Commons
  - ✓ Knowledge Commons
  - ✓ Cultural Commons
  - ✓ Neighborhood Commons
  - ✓ Infrastructure Commons
  - ✓ Global Commons
  - ✓ Market as a Commons
  - ✓ Innovation Commons

- Multi-actor collaborative action
- Coproduction of knowledge and solutions
- Governance and self-governance
- Trust, cooperation and relationship
- Generating and Sharing Value
- Development and autonomy

*Source: Authors (2018)*

The evolution to a knowledge society is still quite challenging and has some characteristics such as (Batra, 2007; Batra & Carrillo, 2015):

- promotion of collaboration rather than competition between economies;

- promotion of sharing rather than protection of knowledge;

- acting in the collective wellbeing of society as a whole and not only in generating economic results;

- understanding that educational achievement is not only a means of economic production, but also a result in itself;

- enhancement of self-realization as well as the ability of individuals to make their own choices based on informed decisions.

If we consider the principles of commons applied to KBD, whose social cohesion is a fundamental element for their reach, and, understanding KBD as a social process of knowledge that generates endogenous value, local potentialities and resources, considering the social, economic and environmental dimensions, in the pursuit of sustainable development (Fachinelli et al., 2014), an analogy can be made between them, as highlighted in table 1.

*Table 1 - Analogy between the principles of Commons (Ostrom, 1990) and the social process of KBD (Fachinelli et al., 2014; Batra & Carrillo, 2015)*

| Principles of Commons (Ostrom, 1990) | The social process of KBD (Fachinelli et al., 2014; Batra & Carrillo, 2015) |
|---|---|
| Clearly defined limits | It considers the unique analysis of a city and cannot be extrapolated to another, concentrates on the strengths and opportunities and on the distinctive aspects of each city. |
| Congruence between appropriation and provision rules and local conditions | Action approaches reflection; establishes a relational and holistic system that combines development, identity, emotional and economic, individual and rational. |
| Collective choice arrangements | It analyses what citizens want to be; part of the existing information and seeks the interpretation that citizens make of it considering their history, personality and emotions. KBD focuses on several collective development alternatives, in which knowledge capital is the strategic medium. |
| Monitoring | Follow up the development based on the Capital System. |
| Mechanisms for sanctions | It provides guidelines for action to citizens. |
| Mechanisms for conflict resolution | Consider what citizens want to carry forward and only what they can carry forward. |
| Recognition of organizational rights | KBD belongs to the citizens and not to the municipal government and therefore transcends the vicissitudes and political changes. |
| Self-governance | The formulation of policies and strategies towards to the knowledge cities underlying KBD are complex procedures that require leadership committed to the sustainable wellbeing of their community to be successful. It also needs a critical mass of change agents with sufficient understanding of qualitative differences in KBD and with the technical capacity to articulate and develop social capital systems. |

*Source: Authors (2018)*

Although the knowledge economy and the knowledge society are increasingly present, the transition from the analysis of the phenomenon to a work structure for the under-standing and development of a knowledge city is still at an early stage (Carrillo & Flores, 2012; Fachinelli et al., 2014). KBD has a method for evaluating and monitoring the capitals of a city: the so-called generic capital system (Carrillo, 2002), presented as a model of knowledge-generation based on value.

Although this work does not intend to approach the capital system, it is important to em-phasize that its objective is to capture all relevant dimensions of value for a social group from a unified system of categories (Carrillo, 2002), and to understand that KBD concen-trates in a series of alternatives for development, in which knowledge capital is the stra-tegic medium (Fachinelli et al., 2014). In this way, Carrillo, Metaxiotis and Yigitcanlar (2010) propose a perspective of KBD in which the accounts of the capital system become an instrument for a balanced, equitable and sustainable development. This view focuses on the equilibrium of collective capital, both intellectual and material (Fachinelli et al., 2014).

Carrillo points out that an epistemological, axiological and political platform that justifies KBD is necessary to allow the mapping and management of its impacts not only in eco-nomic terms, but also in all the main dimensions of social value (Carrillo, Metaxiotis, & Yigitcanlar, 2010).

The evolution of the concept of city over time, compared to the evolution of commons, demonstrates the underlying need to seek a more just, balanced and sustainable society (Figure 2). There are some definitions about cities. Lara et al (2016) presents a framework with domains, with the key issues in smart cities (adapted from Nam and Pardo 2011). For intelligent city, the conceptions focus on infrastructure and ICTs with key issues as smart, mobile, virtual and digital technologies; for the knowledge city the conception is for cre-ative economy and knowledge-based on society with the key issues of entrepreneurship, innovation, competitively and knowledge society.

The understanding that commons is the "shared heritage of all of us" is central to the new commons literature (Hess, 2008). Threats of enclosure have awakened many people to protect common assets beyond the understanding that resources that were once safe as public goods do not require vigilance and even participatory management to safeguard them for the future. For some, commons are a birth right, others recognize the role of personal responsibility in the sustainability of common goods, but the definition of com-mon goods varies with the type of resource available (Hess, 2008).

On the other hand, the knowledge city is a place where new knowledge is constantly created, has excellence in research, supports a flow of new knowledge, constantly invests in the development of human capital and attracts qualified immigrants, in addition to being prone to several types of innovation: technological, organizational and institutional. Therefore, the knowledge city provides an environment of incentive to the generation, dissemination and use of knowledge in an environmentally sustainable, socially fair, economically secure and well-integrated human capital system (Ergazakis, Metaxiotis, & Psarras, 2006; Yigitcanlar, O'Connor, & Westerman, 2008; Fachinelli et al., 2014).

However, the formulation of policies and strategies towards knowledge cities underlying the KBD are still complex procedures that require leadership committed to the sustainable well being of their community in order to be successful (Carrillo & Batra, 2012). In addition, there is also a need for a critical mass of change agents with enough understanding of the qualitative differences in KBD and with the technical capacity to articulate and develop social capital systems.

Open data has also transformed the Smart Cities model. With open data, citizens can develop applications that will provide new services to the city. However, there are still few tangible examples of companies that have successfully transformed city's open data platform to generate profitable apps or related services (M. Lee, E. Almirall, and J. Wareham, 2012).

For Cohen, Almirall and Chesbrough (2016), there is still a need for new business models to drive the effective use of open data within cities. Open data is an excellent example of using a platform to convey third-party capability through common data. They consider that smart cities are a place of opportunity for creating new value for people within the city, and at the same time, can be the locus of serious breaches of trust where information can be shared to provide value to others, while simultaneously harming the city's residents.

However, we can find examples of physical asset mobilization rather than virtual assets. A good example is fab labs and public co-working spaces that allow the involvement of third parties such as developers, artists, manufacturers, and universities. In this case, physical infrastructures operating as commons permit and trigger the participation of an entire ecosystem (Cohen, Almirall, and Chesbrough, 2016).

Beckwith, Sherry and Prendergast (2019) believe that a city should manage its data as a common good, and to this end one must try to understand the potential data flows and values of communities within the city, while respecting legitimate property claims and rules of stewardship. "If cities do this, they can expect that the citizens of the intelligent city will be better served by the intelligent city itself and will be more heavily invested in its success" (Beckwith, Sherry and Prendergast, 2019 p. 219).

## 7. Discussion and Conclusion

Study of the commons and the new commons is a recent, rich and challenging area of research. Some new commons, among them the urban commons, are created, as there are threats of privatization and enclosure in detriment of the social welfare of a particular community. The commons, in this sense, can be understood as a key element to create new economic forms of life, which in turn are increasingly demanded by the challenges of modern life, especially in cities. Commons elements such as self-governance, coproduction of knowledge through collective action, value generation, and sharing require a dynamic and dialectical process that KBD has demonstrated to pursue, a process that demands leadership committed above all to sustainable well-being of their community (Gonzalez et al., 2005).

How can the commons theory contribute to KBD without exhausting the potential contributions of commons? Although the literature on KBD is still recent, it is constructed through social technologies that use the participation and engagement of social actors in a given territory or city, as a social process involving various strategies of economic, societal, spatial development and institutional - to promote, attract and retain investment and talent to form places of life, work, study and visit (Yigitcanlar & Bulu, 2015).

As the open data is considered as new commons, it is so important to improve the knowledge economic development as a raw material for the development of software and applications that contribute to the development of cities, generating entrepreneurship and contributing to the innovation ecosystem. Niaros (2016) demonstrates that a commons-oriented smart city is one that allows for open participation and has mechanisms for resolving democratic problems. To this end, the active participation of society in decision-making processes is essential to create a direct link between technology and community needs.

One of the conceptual challenges of considering open data as a commons is the 'owner-ship' of data. Beckwith, Sherry and Prendergast (2019) consider that data are often created at points of interaction between multiple actors, each of whom has the potential to claim ownership. The data, therefore, usually have property claims distributed by various parties, and dealing with this, considers Beckwith, Sherry and Prendergast (2019) are one of the roles of an intelligent city. For the authors, the great challenge lies in the use of open data as a commons, respecting ownership issues and generating a climate of trust in the community.

The evolution of the field of Knowledge Management (KM) led to the expansion of focus and the application of the principles of knowledge management to promote knowledge-based development (KBD), the third generation of KM. KBD has three interdependent purposes necessary for sustainable and successful development strategies: economic prosperity, human development and social and environmental sustainability (Lazlo & Lazlo, 2007; Carrillo, 2014).

It has a multidisciplinary nature, uses social and economic constructs and its success depends on a committed leadership, especially with the sustainable wellbeing of its community (Laszlo & Laszlo, 2007; Carrillo, 2015).

Considering the complexity of the social and economic constructs used by KBD as development, democracy, government, market, property, sustainability, knowledge, among others, and the emergence of new commons, tangible in social networks, crowdsourcing, open systems, intelligence collective, innovation, entrepreneurship, etc., it becomes apparent that the creation of real or virtual collective spaces the commons theory contributes to KBD as a knowledge field.

The main contributions of the commons are in the processes of value creation and coproduction of knowledge with management of social conflicts; in the vision of sustainability from mechanisms of monitoring and self-governance; in the sharing of content, experiences and skills of individuals, organizations, networks and informal groups, in matters of interest to the city, neighbourhoods or regions, dedicated to the creation of a sustainable society. Considering that a commons is a resource that the community has to take care of, the community needs to be concerned with sustainability and equity and should, also in the case of data resources, implement data governance procedures to ensure this.

It is of course necessary to broaden the discussion and studies on the contribution of commons and new commons to KBD, addressing the impact of scientific, educational, tourism, legal commons, among others. It is also important develop new approaches based on commons to aggregate participation and collective action mechanisms into the KBD field of study, as in the development of common projects, and the analysis of complex problems in planning (e.g. development of frameworks such as Institutional Analysis and Development).

The authors suggest future research that may characterize commons as drivers of knowledge-based development. Considering therefore that the open data promote innovation, entrepreneurship and contribute to an innovation ecosystem. Commons, through open data, can benefit society in the face of the needs of its people.

# 8. References

Beckwith R., Sherry J., Prendergast D. (2019). Data Flow in the Smart City: Open Data Versus the Commons. In: de Lange M., de Waal M. (eds) *The Hackable City*. Springer, Singapore.

Berkes, F., Feeny, D., Mccay, B., & Acheson, J. (1989). The Benefits of the Commons. *Nature, 340*.

Carrillo, F. (2014). What 'knowledge-based' stands for? A position paper. *Journal of Knowledge-Based Development, 5*.

Carrillo, F. (2015). Knowledge-based development as a new economic culture. *Journal of Open Innovation: Technology, Market, and Complexity, 1*.

Carrillo, F. J. (2002). Capital Systems: Implications for a global knowledge agenda. *Journal of Knowledge Management, 6*, pp. 379-399.

Carrillo, F. J. (2004). Capital Cities: A taxonomy of capital accounts for knowledge cities. *Journal of Knowledge Management, 8*, pp. 28-46.

Carrillo, F. J., & Batra, S. (2012). Understanding and measurement: perspectives on the evolution of knowledge-based development. International. *Journal of Knowledge-Based Development, 3*.

Carrillo, F. J., Yigitcanlar, T., Garcia, B., & Lonnqvist, A. (2014). Knowledge and the City: Concepts, Applications and Trends of Knowledge-Based Urban Development. *Routledge Studies in Human Geography*.

Carrillo, F., Metaxiotis, K., & Yigitcanlar, T. (2010). Urban, regional, national and global knowledge capital. (G. Editorial, Ed.) *Journal of Knowledge Management, 14*, pp. 631-634.

Cohen, B., Almirall, E, and Chesbrough, H. (2016). The City as a Lab:Open Innovation Meets the Collaborative Economy. *California Management Review*, Vol. 59(1) 5–13.

Denzin, N.K. and Lincoln, Y.S. (1994), Handbook of Qualitative Research, Sage, Thousand Oaks, CA

Errichiello, L., & Marasco, A. (2014). Open service innovation in smart cities: A framework for exploring innovation networks in the development of new city services. *Advanced Engineering Forum*, 11, 115–124.

Ergazakis, K., Metaxiotis, K., & Psarras, J. (2006). Knowledge cities: The answer to the needs of knowledge-based development. *VINE: The Journal of Information and Knowledge Management Systems, 36*, pp. 67-84.

Fachinelli, A. C., Carrillo, F. J., & D'Arisbo, A. (2014). Capital system, creative economy and knowledge city transformation: Insights from Bento Gonçalves, Brazil. *Expert Systems with Applications*, pp. 5614-5624.

Ferreira, S., & Neto, M. (2005). Knowledge Management and Social Learning: Exploring the *Cognitive Dimension of Development. 1, 3*, 4-17. Retrieved from http://www.km4dev.org/journal: http://www.km4dev.org/journal

Foster, S. (2013). Collective Action and the Urban Commons. *Notre Dame Law Review, 87*. Retrieved from http://scholarship.law.nd.edu/ndlr/vol87/iss1/2

Frischmann, B., Madison, M., & Strandburg, K. (2014). Introduction & Chapter. In M. J. Brett M. Frischmann, *Governing Knowledge Commons.* Oxford University Press.

Gonzalez, M., Alvarado, J., & Martinez, S. (2005). A compilation of resources on knowledge cities and knowledge-based development. *Journal of Knowledge Management, 8*, pp. 107-127.

Harvey, D. (2011). The Future of the Commons. *Radical History Review, 109*, pp. 101-107. Retrieved February 19, 2018, from https://read.dukeupress.edu/radical-history-review/article/2011/109/101/75136/The-Future-of-the-Commons

Harvey, D. (2012). Rebel Cities: From the Right to the City to the Urban Revolution. New York. Retrieved February 2018, from http://abahlali.org/files/Harvey_Rebel_cities.pdf

Hess, C. (2005). The Comprehensive Bibliography of the Commons. (T. d. commons, Ed.) Retrieved from http://dlc.dlib.indiana.edu/dlc/

Hess, C. (2008). Mapping the New Commons. *12th Biennial Conference of the International Association for the Study of the Commons.* Cheltenham, England: HESS, C. Mapping the New Commons. 12th Biennial Conference of the International Association fo University of Gloucestershire. Retrieved from https://papers.ssrn.com/sol3/papers.cfm?abstract

Hess, C., & Ostrom, E. (2007). A Framework for Analyzing the Knowledge Commons. In E. b. Ostrom, *Understanding Knowledge as a Commons: From Theory to Practice* (pp. 41-81). Cambridge: MIT Press.

Huron, A. (2012). The work of the urban commons: limited-equity cooperatives in Washington, D.C. Graduate Faculty in Earth and Environmental Sciences.

Knight, R. (1995). Knowledge-based development: policy and planning implications for cities. *Urban Studies, 32*, pp. 225-260.

Lara, A., Da Costa, E., Furlani, T. Z., & Yigitcanlar, T. (2016). Smartness that matters: towards a comprehensive and human-centred characterisation of smart cities. *Journal of Open Innovation: Technology, Market, and Complexity, 2*.

Laszlo, K. C., & Laszlo, A. (2007). Fostering a Sustainable Learning Society through Knowledge Based Development. *Systems Research and Behavioral Science. Syst. Res.*, pp. 493-503.

M. Lee, E. Almirall, and J. Wareham, "Open Data and Civic Apps: First-Generation Failures, Second-Generation Improvements," Communications of the ACM, 59/1 (January

2016): 82-89; M. Janssen, Y. Charalabidis, and A. Zuiderwijk, "Benefits, Adoption Barriers and Myths of Open Data and Open Government," *Information Systems Management*, 29/4 (2012): 258-268.

Madison, M., Frischmann, B., & Strandburg, K. (2010). Constructing Commons in the Cultural Environment. *Cornell Law Review, 95*, pp. 657-709.

Madison, M., Strandburg, K. J., & Frischmann, B. (2015). Knowledge Commons. In P. M. Schwartz (Ed.), *Forthcoming, Research Handbook on the Economics of Intellectual Property Law* (Vols. Vol. II – Analytical Methods). Edward Elgar Publishing.

Niaros, V. (2016). Introducing a taxonomy of the "smart city": Towards a commons-oriented approach? tripleC: Communication, capitalism & critique. *Open Access Journal for a Global Sustainable Information Society*, 14, 51–61.

Nightingale, A. (2011). Beyond design principles: Subjectivity, emotion, and the (Non)rational commons. *Society and Natural Resources, 24*, pp. 119-132.

Ostrom, E. (1990). *Governing the Commons: The evolution of institutions for collective action.* (I. University, Ed.) Cambridge University Press.

Ostrom, E. (1995). Self-organization and Social Capital. *Industrial and Corporate Change, 4*, pp. 131-159.

Ostrom, E. (1996). The Great Divide: Coproduction, Synergy, and Development. *World Development, 24*, pp. 1073-1087.

Ostrom, E. (1998). A Behavioral Approach to the Rational Choice Theory of Collective Action: Presidential Address, American Political Science Association. *The American Political Science Review, 92*, pp. 1-22.

Ostrom, E., & HESS, C. (2007). A Framework for Analyzing the Knowledge Commons. In C. H. Ostrom (Ed.), *Understanding Knowledge as a Commons: From Theory to Practice.* MIT Press.

Pittaway, L., Robertson, M., Munir, K., Denyer, D., Neely, A. (2004). Networking and innovation: a systematic review of the evidence", International Journal of Management Reviews, Vol. 5, No. 3-4, pp. 137-168.

Sampaio, C. A., & Fernandes, V. (2006, jul/dez). Formulação de Estratégias de Desenvolvimento Baseado no Conhecimento Local. *RAE- Eletrônica. [online], 5*. Retrieved from http://rae.fgv.br/sites/rae.fgv.br/files/artigos/

Thompson, R. J. (2014). Commoning; creating a new socio-economic order? A grounded theory study. *PhD Thesis at faculty of Fielding Graduate University.*

Yigitcanlar, T. (2010). Making space and place for the knowledge economy: knowledge-based development of Australian cities. *European Planning Studies, 18*, pp. 1769-1786.

Yigitcanlar, T. (2011). Knowledge-based urban development redefined: from theory to practice knowledge-based development of cities. In T. &. Yigitcanlar (Ed.), *Summit Proceedings of the 4th Knowledge Cities World Summit* (pp. 389-399). Bento Gonçalves, Brazil: The World Capital Institute and Ibero-American Community for Knowledge Systems.

Yigitcanlar, T., & Bulu, M. (2015). Dubaization of Istanbul: Insights from the knowledge-based urban development journey of an emerging local economy. *Environment & Planning A, 47*, pp. 89-107. doi:10.1068/a130209p

Yigitcanlar, T., Edvardssonb, I. R., Johannessonc, H., Kamruzzamana, M., Ioppolod, G., & Pancholia, S. (2017). Knowledge-based development dynamics in less favoured regions: insights from Australian and Icelandic university towns. *European Planning Studies*.

Yigitcanlar, T., O'Connor, K., & Westerman, C. (2008). The making of knowledge cities: Melbourne's knowledge-based urban development experience. *Cities, 25*, pp. 63-72.

Yigitcanlar, T., Kamruzzaman, M., Buys. L., Ioppollo, G., Sabatini -Marques, J., Costa, E., (2018). Understanding 'smart cities': Intertwining development drivers with desired outcomes in a multidimensional framework. *Cities*, 81, 145–160.

Yigitcanlar, T., Kamruzzaman, M., Foth, M., Sabatini-Marques, J., Costa, E., & Ioppolo, G., (2019). Can cities become smart without being sustainable? A systematic review of the literature. *Sustainable Cities and Society*, 45(1), 348-365.

# Living up to a Universal Social Contract

*Elly Rijnierse*

## 1. Introduction

The Economy for the Common Good approach, which does not aim to incorporate sustainability into the predominant rationale of profit-maximization but to embed economic activities into a broader cultural and social context and to link them with the core human values of dignity, solidarity, social justice, environmental sustainability, democracy and transparency (ECGPW 2019), provides the frame for this paper. The key objective is to discuss whether a global common focus on 'Living up to a Universal Social Contract' can provide a pathway for the Economy for the Common Good to emerge.

A Social Contract can be defined as "an implicit agreement among the members of a society to cooperate for social benefits" (Oxford dictionary). If an Economy for the Common Good is aspired to at a global level, then it becomes necessary to be able to imagine a Universal Social Contract among all members of the global society, in which a social contract between citizens and the State is only one building block. To this end basic typologies of governance, including context specific dynamics of parallel functioning governance systems at the local, national and transnational level, will be discussed.

It is suggested that at the level of the United Nations the main features of a Universal Social Contract have already been signed by means of the adoption of the Sustainable Development Goals (SDGs) in 2015, which set the objectives and the collective responsibility to achieve a better and more sustainable future for all. The SDGs address global challenges and it is underlined that they are all interconnected. Equally at the level of the United Nations the Universal Declaration of Human Rights (UDHR) has been signed in 1948. The SDGs and the UDHR create the pillars of both the *structure* (common goals, common responsibility) and *actor* (human rights) perspective, the two elements that constitute a system. In between these two pillars numerous declarations and conventions have been signed, including those addressing the social foundations and the ecological ceiling of our planet. Doughnut Economics (Raworth 2017, 45) has defined itself as operating between these foundations and this ceiling. A Universal Social Contract entails the Common Good as a leading principle. This relationship requires further elaboration.

As a kick-off for this discussion, the question for this paper is: *What kind of governance modalities are required to be able to live up to the Universal Social Contract and how can these governance modalities realistically be created*? This question addresses both the structure -, or system perspective (top-down), as it asks what governance structures are required, as well as the actor perspective (bottom-up). This question is addressed in this paper in the realm of discussions among practitioners in the field of climate adaptation in the Sahel and starts from the bottom-up perspective, the actor's perspective.

A vision on what might be effective governance structures and - dynamics for the realization of the Universal Social Contract and how to get there emerges from the present study on the governance of the Landscape Approach in the Sahel Region, which is aimed at facing the challenge of Climate Change. The perspective of local communities, who's livelihoods are threatened by degraded land and water resources caused or aggravated by climate change, is put first. The more specific question fitting in this field is: *Under which conditions, in terms of governance, investments in landscape restoration actually can create opportunities for local producers in the Sahel, and communities at large, to build sustainable and productive livelihoods and resilience to an increasingly uncertain climate, which then in turn may contribute to stability and sustainable development in the region?* The exploration of this question leads to the development of a theory of change at community level (actor) and a theory of change at the collective, global level (structure). By following both Theories of Change on governance modalities a system change could occur which facilitates the emergence of the Economy for the Common Good.

Mali, and especially the Inner Niger Delta in the Mopti Region, is highlighted as a case, because of the decennia long history of national and international investments and engagement in democratisation and food-security as well as the recent instability in the region and the renewed European international policy focus on this region.

First the governance challenges as faced by local communities in the Sahel are depicted. Then the debate on conflicting governance structures is framed along the lines of three basic families of political discourse, each with its own rationale and consequent governance structures. It is argued that the three basic typologies of governance structures co-exist in virtually every locality, sometimes functional, sometimes dysfunctional, thus leading to tensions, conflict or environmental degradation. Following the logic of the Landscape Approach and the Human Security Approach, both non-state centered approaches aligned with the Sustainable Development Goals and the Universal Human Rights, a Theory of Change towards governance for Stability, Peace and Sustainable Development at community level is designed, as well as a Theory of Change at global system level.

It will be concluded that, in order to collectively live up to a Universal Social Contract, communities need to have a legitimate and legally protected place at the negotiation table for sustainable development of their locality, which then allows for the creation of Public-Private-Peoples Partnerships (PPPPs) rather than Public-Private Partnerships (PPPs). In that capacity communities and civil society at large are the drivers of positive change towards an Economy for the Common Good, were profit oriented activities are embedded into a broader cultural and social context and are linked to the core human values. This may imply a paradigm shift regarding the primary role of the State from the facilitation of capital accumulation and the redistribution of wealth, a main feature of the current West - European welfare state, to the facilitation of self-organization and the creation of social and environmental value for the common good. This may allow for participatory, far more resilient and interconnected societies to emerge. Simultaneously a global paradigm shift in this sense may diminishing space for predatory leadership, with high levels of political power and economic discretion and low levels of public investment, as both local economies tend to flourish and transnational reflexive democracy structures and institutions may help to counter abuse and may support the fulfillment of basic needs.

## 2. Landscape Degradation in the Sahel and the Need to Invest

The West African Sahel and Dry Savannas stretch from Mauritania in the west through southern Mali, northern Ghana, Burkina Faso, southern Niger, and northern Nigeria to Chad in the east. It comprises a vast mosaic of rangelands, forests and agricultural land linked and integrated by wetlands such as rivers, inland floodplains, lakes, swamps. In this vast region, frequent droughts, poor water management, increasing use of marginal lands, overgrazing (resulting in conflicts between farmers and stock farmers), weak policies and institutions, extreme poverty and a growing population have led to depleted soils and degradation of natural resources. Rural livelihoods are under constant threat of famine as shifting cultivation has become impossible and areas of rangelands, wetlands and forests are continuously shrinking. In the dryer northern part between the desert and the savannas, the main challenge is to restore degraded ecosystems. In the southern part, where agricultural support services and access to markets tend to be better than in the north, the challenge is to sustainably intensify agricultural production based on the sound ecological conditions (CGIAR 2018).

| |
|---|
| *Land degradation in drylands* |
| 44% of global food production takes place in the world's degrading drylands |

> 12 million hectares of soil are lost each year from desertification and drought alone, whereas 20 million tons of grain could have grown instead. (Noel, Mukulcak, Stewart. & Etter 2015, 8)

The link between land degradation and instability has been investigated in recent years (Van Schaik 2014). Competition over different natural systems and their productivity can intensify and exacerbate existing tensions, enhance the risk for conflict, regional and international migration and potentially contribute to crime or extremism (Barbut and Alexander 2015, 6).

There is need for investment in landscape restoration in order to roll back this chain. The question is: which kind of investments and under what kind of governance structures? 'Business as usual' will probably lead to 'results as usual'. Landscape degradation is caused by a dominant view of maximization of Return on Investment (RoI) per hectare (Ferwerda 2015). In the field of Landscape Restoration the Landscape Governance Approach is emerging in order to create to conditions for new forms of investment.

> *Landscape Restoration* is the process of assisting the recovery of entire ecosystems within a landscape that have been degraded, damaged or destroyed (Ferwerda 2016, 84).
>
> An *Ecosystem* is the complex of living organisms, their physical environment, and all their relationships in a particular unit of space (Britannica 2018).
>
> A *Landscape Approach* sets a framework that promotes integrated planning and the creation of partnerships, all with the aim of achieving sustainability in the landscape in the broadest sense (Mbow, Neely and Dobie 2015). "Landscape approaches" seek to provide tools and concepts for allocating and managing land to achieve social, economic, and environmental objectives in areas where agriculture, mining, and other productive land uses compete with environmental and biodiversity goals (Sayer et al. 2013).
>
> *Landscape Governance* generally refers to a place-based multi-stakeholder process of negotiation and spatial decision-making within its wider institutional context, with the aim to maintain, enhance or restore the landscape's functions, goods and services in a long-lasting manner (Van Oosten, Gunarso, Koesoetjahjo and Wiersum 2014).

# 3. Towards Trust-based Global Governance: Bottom-Up Perspective

This paper builds upon studies on governance in the Sahel Region, more specifically in the Inner Niger Delta in Mopti Region in Mali. From the viewpoint of local communities, local governance as it has emerged historically can be viewed as 'structural chaos' (Ursu 2018). It is suggested that landscape governance has the capacity to gradually overcome this 'structural chaos' bottom-up.

## 3.1 History and Context

'Given the [governance] conditions under which local producers in the Sahel are obliged to work, they are doing extremely well' (Van Dijk 2018). However, the current overall trend is a loss of livelihood opportunities, partly as a consequence of ecosystem degradation. What are the barriers for local producers to build sustainable and productive livelihoods?

Governance structures evolve over centuries in relation to the physical environment, livelihood strategies, religion, culture, tenure and identities, and encounters with external interventions, such as regional and tribal conflicts, colonization, international cooperation and foreign investment (United Nations Environmental Program 2012). Every single area has a specific history, which is essential to understand in order to build a vision for the future.

An example is the Inner Niger Delta in Mali which is described as 'a contested space' (Ursu 2018). An historical analysis of the governance system in the Mopti region shows how colonial rule has destabilized a natural resources management system, which was meticulously build in the 19th century. The consequent 'organized chaos' has aggravated after independence, despite numerous state building interventions such as decentralization policies in the 1980s and 1990s. This institutional chaos has created space for radical armed groups to settle in.

---

*Casus: Governance Mali – Inner Niger Delta* (Ursu 2018)
Between the 9th and 16th centuries, the area was incorporated within the great West African trading empires in control of the north-south axis of trans-Saharan commerce. The main products exchanged along this route were salt, manufactured goods, gold and slaves.

---

Between 1820 and 1862, the entire inner Delta was unified into a theocratic Muslim state known as the Dina, or Macina Empire, under the rule of the Fulani marabout Sékou Amadou. He created a complex natural resources management system to end the numerous intra-ethnic conflicts among Fulani populations and to regulate access and use of resources in the Inner Niger Delta. This system of governance was built on existing norms of allocation and management of natural resources that date back to early history. Drawing on principles of Islam, the Dina led to nomadic populations becoming sedentary, regulated the seasonal movement of herds, and divided resources between pastoral (nomadic) and agricultural (sedentary) groups. Perhaps one of the most important transformations brought about by the Dina was the centralized management of access and use of resources that represented a shift of power from nomadic to sedentary groups. The centralized administration was overseen by the Dina Council in Hamdullahi, linking agricultural, pastoral and fishing activities across production systems and ethnic lines.

The Dina did not last long, since it was overthrown by new competitors, including French troops that colonized the region between 1894 and 1960. Customary law and traditional political structures have been structurally undermined by colonial rule. These imbalances in the system have not been redressed by the national governments after independence. Traditional leaders have been deprived of law enforcing powers, while the State has not managed to install legitimate alternatives. The added competing and overlapping state institutions have rather contributed to the creation of a governance system characterized by 'structural chaos'.

In current times this is the fertile breeding ground for the settlement of armed radical groups. The main source of conflict in the Sahel region is access to land and other natural resources among competing socio-professional groups, often, but not always, along ethnic lines. Formal justice is perceived as expensive, lengthy, corrupt, unaware of local dynamics and abusive, while customary justice is lacking enforcement powers and state support to implement decisions that can prevent the escalation of conflict. Radical armed groups have entered this vacuum by providing ánd reinforcing conflict solutions, often in favour of those who are historically marginalized.

From the point of view of a local farmer, experiencing the consequences of the power struggles over the institutions and resources and the chaos and insecurity that emerge from there, it is difficult to appreciate national, regional and international institutions and policies to counter desertification in the region.

Nonetheless, it cannot be denied that enormous effort and knowledge have been and are being put into realizing food security in the region. Following severe droughts in the region, the Inter-State Committee for Drought Control in the Sahel (CILSS) was set up in 1973. End 1990's, the Desert Margin Initiative (UNCCD) was one of the first transnational initiatives to combat desertification and increase livelihood (Koala and Van Duivenbooden 1999). In 2001 the Sahel and West Africa Club (SWAC) emerged from the Club du Sahel in 1976. The SWAC, with the Organisation for Economic Cooperation and Development (OECD) hosting the secretariat, provides a platform for dialogue to improve regional governance on food and nutrition security and to improve understanding of transformation in the region and their policy implications (OECD 2018).

More specifically landscape restoration initiatives are already implemented since the early 1980s. These initiatives were strengthened amongst others through the Bonn Challenge in 2011, setting the goal for the Global Partnership on Forest and Landscape Restoration (GPFLR). The Bonn Challenge aims to realize many existing commitments, such as the Convention on Biological Diversity (CBD), the United Nations Framework Convention on Climate Change (UNFCCC) REDD+ goal and the Rio+20 targets. This in turn paved the way for regional initiatives such as AFR100, Triple S (3S) and the Great Green Wall Initiative (Van Schaik, Kamphof and Sarris 2018, 19). However, in view of the noted tendencies in terms of degrading drylands and increasing instability, it looks like a machinery of which the engine fails to start.

*Barriers for local producers*
If the above sketches roughly the political - institutional history, the current governance context and future prospects in a way that is exemplary for the Sahel, what are then the challenges a local farmer, fisherman or herder, women and men, face if they are to build a sustainable and productive livelihood?

*Insecurity* blocks everything. Securing safety for the producers is primordial to create space for building sustainable and productive livelihoods. However, who is intervening on behalf of whom, and to what end? What is the impact of interventions on governance structures in the future?
*The number of development policies*, including landscape restoration programmes, is dazzling. The funding infrastructure behind the multiple initiatives even more. Again, who is funding what, and whose interests are served, based on which values and principles? How can a simple farmer capitalize on investment, when the elephants fight and the grass gets trampled?

Given the current *conflicting and competing governance institutions* - the traditional, the national and the transnational institutions -, local producers have to negotiate with local traditional leaders, opinion makers, local and national government, international institutions and investors to secure land tenure for example or get access to information. Positioning oneself in this sense becomes an individual, pragmatic and highly complex strategy.

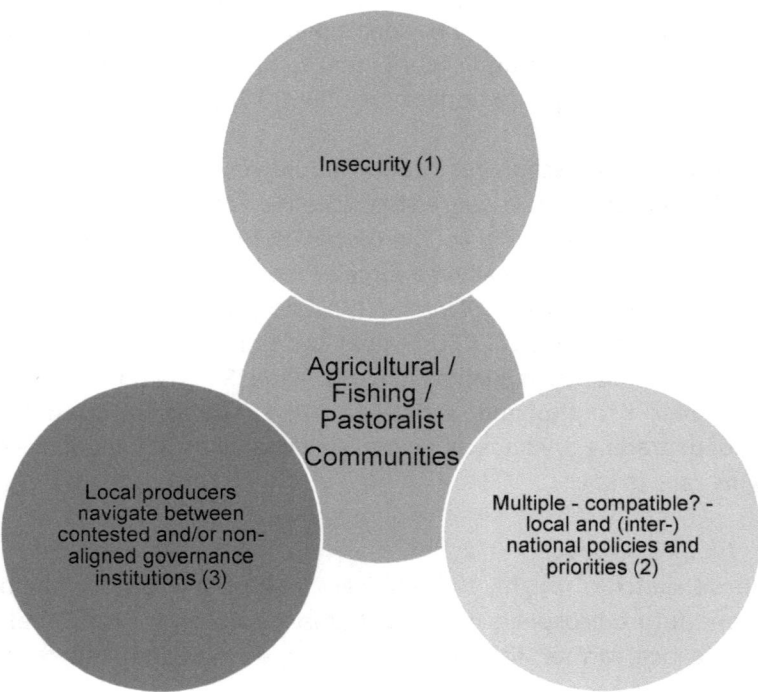

*Figure 1: Barriers for local communities to build sustainable and productive livelihoods*

A clear common outlook for all stakeholders – if only in the long-term - is necessary in order to build towards trust, collaboration and system transformation. It may be safe to conclude that a simple farmer, fisherman or herder, a simple man or woman in the Inner Niger Delta region in Mali will not be able to overcome these barriers, if there are no structural changes in the governance system creating conditions in which he or she can operate meaningfully.

*Structuring the analysis along the lines of families of political discourse*
A specific context is difficult to assess, as is shown with the case of the Inner Niger Delta, the Mopti region. Even more difficult is to agree among different stakeholders about steps to be taken.

A way of working with the complexity is understanding the context through a lens of contested political spaces. With this lens one can 'travel' through institutions, from the local to the global level, in time and in space. It provides a compass.

Political spaces are created by visions about the way people imagine how society should be organized. The political philosopher Pieter Boele van Hensbroek developed a 'grammar of modern African political thought', in which he summarized three basic families of discourse: Identity, Modernization and Liberalization (Boele van Hensbroek 1998, 160). These families happen to coincide with the three values of the French Revolution: Fraternité, Egalité, Liberté (Figure 2) (Rijnierse 2000). This may well be the place where African and European political philosophy meet, and hence offer an opportunity to create a conceptual space for dialogue and mutual understanding.

The *Identity discourse* has shaped traditional institutions - or vice versa -, in a context of subsistence economy and rivalling ethnic groups, with Brotherhood as the dominant value.

The *Modernisation discourse* is primarily embodied in the State. The Modernisation discourse thrived during the industrial revolution. Equality is the dominant value in the welfare state, that has been built with the extraordinary revenues generated by industrialization, while extracting fossil fuels.

The *Liberation discourse* is upcoming – and highly contested - with globalization. The liberation discourse is manifested in organisations and institutions, primarily focussing on basic human needs, working from the local to the global level, with Freedom as the dominant value.

Brotherhood, Equality and Freedom are concepts that have different meanings in different contexts. If one is dominant in a certain context, it defines the meaning of the others in the same context (Boele van Hensbroek 1998). In the Liberation discourse, Freedom as Development (Sen 1999) is a widely adopted definition.

In the current times of globalization, one can safely claim that in any specific context the three discourses are present and materialized in existing – often highly contested – institutions and policies, as shown in the case of the Inner Niger Delta in Mali.

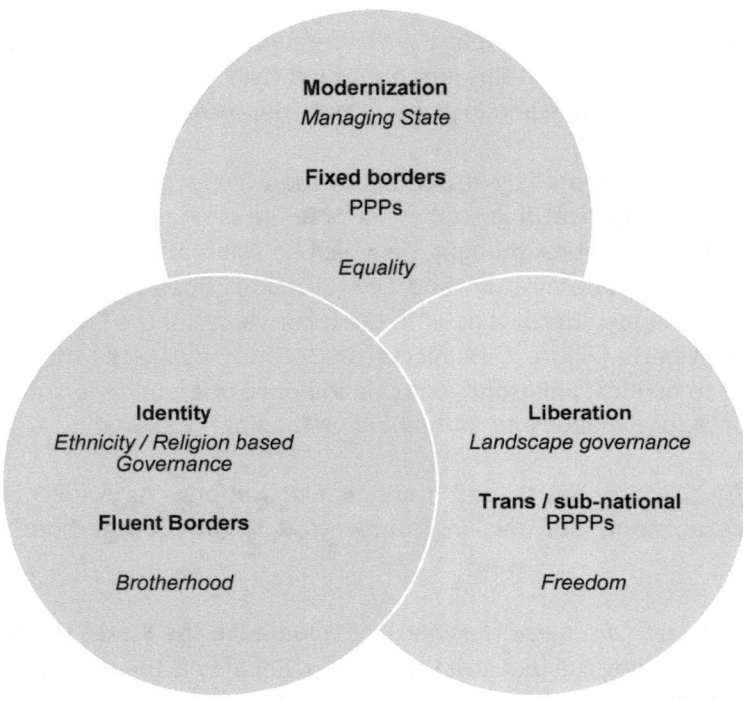

*Figure 2: Three families of discourse – conceptual common ground*

As Figure 2 illustrates, discourses materialize in institutions and policies. The triangle in the middle represents the space where these institutions co-exist. This can be a functional balance between discourses, hence between institutions with different leading principles. In the Malian case the configuration of institutions and political spaces is the result of historical and present power struggles and highly contested.

### 3.2 How to overcome barriers bottom-up?

After taking stock of the conflicting paradigms and how they play out in a specific case such as the Inner Niger Delta, identifying a common focus for sustainable development in this area is crucial for alignment and building trust between diverse actors for collective action.

Aligning diverse local interests with national and transnational policies and investments from the bottom-up is amongst others possible by putting local ecosystems, including all actors depending on the natural resources in that area, at the centre of the analysis and policy making. This is the starting point of Landscape Approaches and Landscape Governance. Key is a territorial approach, in which the borders are determined by an ecosystem and thus not necessarily coincide with administrative borders.

*Strengthening local ownership through strengthening governance capabilities*
While the foregoing part dealt with the political and institutional aspects, another key factor is the ownership of landscape development by local people. Without local ownership development will never last. This is why investment in soft skills should be part and parcel of the Landscape governance.

Landscape governance involves all aspects of the ecosystem, including building a sustainable economy which is based upon a long-term vision, as well as anticipating upcoming challenges in the future. This leads to a shift in focus away from technical aspects of landscape restoration to landscape governance. In order to achieve widescale sustainable impact in reversing land degradation, a drastic change in strategy is needed: one that empowers farmers to be responsible stewards of resilient farms. The same goes for fishing and herding. However, fostering this resilience-based stewardship requires a significant change in mind-set, both among farmers, policymakers and investors (Kessler and Van Reemst 2018). Therefore, support and space for the development of 'soft skills' across communities, authorities, donors and investors alike are required to be able to implement collectively bottom up, participatory and adaptive special planning processes.

*Theory of Change: bottom-up institutional alignment through Landscape Governance*
A *Theory of Change* for overcoming bottom-up barriers for local producers and community at large to build sustainable and productive livelihoods through Landscape Governance may look as follows:

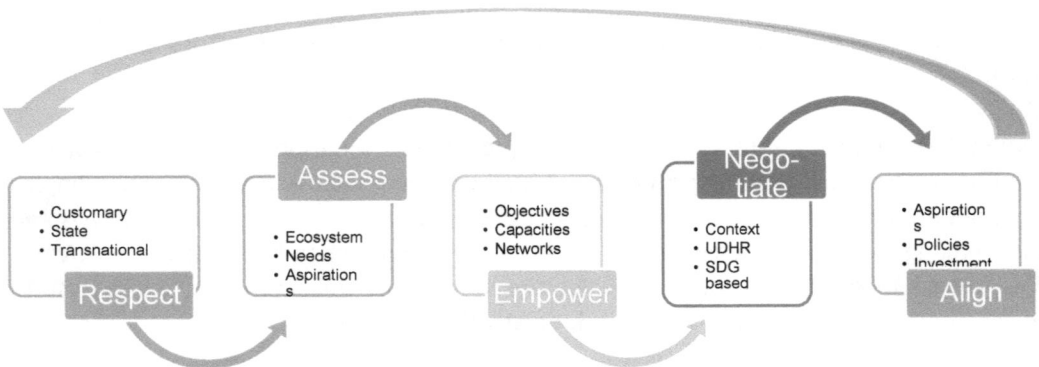

*Figure 3: Theory of Change: Landscape Governance for Sustainable Development*

The Theory of Change needs to be read as an ongoing circle, through which over the years progressively good Landscape Governance is build and the resilience of the landscape and the local communities grow.

This Theory of Change starts from the 'State of the Art', that is a situation where multiple visions on governance are present among the participants and participating organisations, entrepreneurs and institutions in the multi-stakeholder fora. It is important to respect these visions and appreciate the diverse positions of the institutions, since they all have a rationale from different viewpoints and backgrounds. It is not likely that these visions and positions will change, unless mutual trust between all stakeholders is built, and a way forward is carved out together.

This Theory of Change is not neutral, it is geared towards the formulation of a shared vision and strategy in a time and space specific contexts under the larger objective of the sustainable management of natural and human resources from the local to the global level. In the realization of the objective to foster an Economy for the Common Good, *oiko-nomia,* (Felber 2017, 25), the State is bound to take a facilitating role, rather than a di-recting role. The drivers of change from bottom-up are the needs and aspirations of the local communities.

In current practice the lack of a shared vision for the future and shared principles on how to proceed leads to policy conflicts, which are played out at the local level. Overcoming the contradictions is left to the individual capabilities of landscape actors, who muddle their way through a myriad of competing and contrasting rules and regulations, which hardly match their interest' (Van Oosten, Runhaar and Arts 2019, 7). In order to sustain and scale up, landscape restoration initiatives should be progressively embedded in governance arrangements, either based on accepted forms of authority, or otherwise landscape governance requires other sources of legitimacy. Examples are informal, yet functional multi-stakeholder and multi-sectoral platforms, partnership or taskforces (Van Oosten, Runhaar and Arts 2019, 7). In literature about the Common Good, different forms of institutions are referred to such as social charters and commonwealth trusts. (Quilligan 2013). Common wealth trusts allow for creating bioregional councils, guilds, entrepreneurial hubs, and strategic planning agencies dedicated to coordinating the efforts of local communities in protecting their ecosystems and ensuring that the resources which belong to everyone actually meet the needs of everyone (Quilligan 2015), while aligning with global goals in the areas of climate change and biodiversity for example.

Within these institutional frames, new capacities of the various stakeholders are needed in order to govern landscapes and achieve concrete results. Based on literature, a survey among landscape practitioners and experiences from other fields, desired *landscape governance capabilities* are identified: those aimed at managing concrete interventions for land restoration or sustainable landscape management (substance), and those capabilities to organize participatory decision-making and policy alignment (process) (Van Oosten, Runhaar and Arts 2019, 18)

---

*Landscape governance capabilities: 'Substance' and 'Process' oriented* (Van Oosten, Runhaar and Arts 2019)

those aimed to 'maintain, enhance or restore a landscape's functions, and the goods and services this it provides (substance) and

those aimed to manage a 'place-based stakeholder process of spatial decision making with a wider institutional context' (process). The latter may be well summarized as 'the ability to creatively combine and stretch rules, policies and regulations through institutional bricolage and entrepreneurship'

---

The definition of process capabilities is interesting in the sense that Landscape Governance requires – by definition – the capability to engage with institutions of different nature and to be creative, since that is the historically grown situation where we are starting from. The desired 'alignment' of institutions is a long-term ideal, good to focus on, but not to be expected in the here and now. 'Substance results' are required in the short term for stability and survival by creatively making use of the diverse existing governance institutions, 'Process results' require patience, imagination, negotiations for governance reform from the local to the global level.

### 3.3 Bottom-up Approach to System Change

This Theory of Change is to be read from the perspective of the individual stakeholder, the local community and local institutions in landscape management. If the individual or the community is not supported by national and transnational governance institutions, based on compatible values and principles, the landscape approach may remain a 'case-by-case', uphill struggle. Yet the system-based approach in the research on landscape governance capabilities makes it 'a systemic process of societal learning, which addresses drivers of degradation, patterns of societal behaviour, issues of power and authority, and (re)distribution of access to and control over a landscape's resources' (Van Oosten, Runhaar and. Arts 2019, 21)

This system-based approach to landscape governance capabilities is associated with the capabilities approach, as developed by Nobel laureate Amarthya Sen, 'in which capabilities are not attributed to individuals as such, but on the deeper development objectives of society underneath'. 'Capabilities', so Sen argues, 'refer to the set of abilities that allow *all* individuals within society to enhance their valuable options – so called freedoms – to choose their destination' (Van Oosten, Runhaar and Arts 2019, 8)

### 3.4 Concerted action through the Human Security Approach

Political instability and civil conflict constitute a risk for foreign investors. Yet, investments in landscape restoration are a crucial investment in peace, security and sustainable development in the Sahel. This dilemma – typical chicken and egg - may be overcome by synchronizing policies towards security and development. The Human Security concept may well serve to make the connection between conventional security policies and investments in long term stability and sustainable development.

The United Nations Commission on Human Security (CHS) re-conceptualizes security by (United Nations 2009, 6-7).
Moving away from traditional, state-centric conceptions of security that focusses primarily on the safety of states from military aggression, to one that concentrates on the security of the individuals, their protection and empowerment

Drawing attention to a multitude of threats that cut different aspects of human life and thus highlighting the interface between security, development and human rights; and Promoting instead a new integrated, coordinated and people-centered approach to advancing peace, security and development within and across nations.

> *Human Security* "...to protect the vital core of all human lives in ways that enhance human freedoms and human fulfilment. Human security means protecting fundamental freedoms – freedoms that are the essence of life. It means protecting people from critical (severe) and pervasive (widespread) threats and situations. It means using processes that build on people's strengths and aspirations. It means creating political, social, environmental, economic, military and cultural systems that together give people the building blocks of survival, livelihood and dignity." (United Nations 2009, 6).

Amarthya Sen participated in the CHS. *The Fundamental Human Freedoms*, derived from his theory 'Development as Freedom', appear as the basis of the Human Security concept. These Freedoms have also been identified as relevant for landscape governance and landscape restoration approaches. Not surprisingly, the operationalization of human security in practice does have similarities with the landscape governance practices, which makes both approaches compatible.

Human security is an interdisciplinary concept, that is people-centred, multi-sectoral, comprehensive, context specific and prevention oriented. Similar governance challenges as in landscape governance are mentioned, such as 'turf war' between organizations and top down, politically motivated grand strategies. Similar solutions are proposed, such as participatory approaches, local capacity building and community empowerment, while allowing for local leadership and feedback from affected communities. The types of human security threats that are identified are *economic security*, *food security*, health security, *environmental security*, personal security, community security and political security (United Nations 2009, 7). This may allow the Human Security Approach to become a 'trait-d'union' between the Landscape Approach and the security issue, which needs to be addressed in order to be able to scale up investments.

*Non-state centred approaches: adaptive governance of complex societal systems*
Both the Human Security Approach and the Landscape Restoration Approach are non-state centred approaches. This does not mean 'by-passing' the state, nor countervailing the state, but it means that governance is organized around human needs and landscape stewardship, involving all stakeholders. No single actor or sector can fulfil all human needs, nor manage the ecosystem. It requires collaboration between all stakeholders, in

time and place specific coalitions. This changes the role of the state institutions from a *managing and providing* role to a *facilitating* role around commonly agreed objectives in a specific physical area. It requires balancing out national and global objectives, as set by climate change agreements for example, and local priorities, while assuring an integrated approach at the local level.

This is a highly complex exercise. It requires a well-organized civil society and a legitimate place of civil society at the negotiation table to set time- and place-specific priorities. Mintzberg pleas for Public-Private-Peoples-Partnerships (PPPPs) for Climate Change the *Plural sector* – civil society in its broadest sense - is added to the equation. In the current situation the Public Sector has the obligation to oversee by orchestrated planning. The *Plural Sector* tends to favor grounded engagement. Businesses, as independent organizations in the marketplace, are most inclined to favor autonomous venturing. In the current understanding of the role of the state, civil society is often experienced as opposing, criticizing. Mintzberg depicts a downward spiral often occurring in the current system, leading to destabilization, social disaggregation and distrust: The Private sector is lobbying the Public Sector =>The Public Sector is policing Civil Society => Civil Society is protesting against the prerogatives and the negative impact of the companies and commercialization. He proposes to turn this downward spiral into an upward spiral through cooperation and turning the direction of action: The Plural Sector is activating the Public Sector => The Public Sector is legislating the Private Sector => The Private Sector is provisioning the Plural Sector (Mintzberg, Etzion and Mantere 2018).

For the Plural Sector to play this role as kick-start of change effectively, legitimately, at scale and in the long run, the Plural Sector may require strengthening of its position through enhanced organization and legal anchoring of the Plural Sector in participatory processes. When linking this to a specific area, defined by an ecosystem, it provides the conditions for horizontal governance structures and area-related financial arrangements. An example of this is being set in the Dutch context by Ravenhorst, Spronck and Van Bekkum. They are developing a Rhineland Area Arrangement model, a PPPP, for integrated area development (Ravenhorst, Spronck and van Bekkum 2018), anticipating a new Dutch law on spacial planning in which an ecosystem based territorial approach is envisioned and participation of local communities is one of the pillars of the law.

Turning the Mintzberg downward cycle into an upward cycle is exactly what Human Security Approach and Landscape Governance may be able to achieve if aligned. A 'bottom-up strategy' can only succeed through a common determination of the Public, the Private and the Plural sector. This requires leadership in all three sectors. The above-mentioned landscape governance capabilities, both process and substance oriented, and the soft skills required for the Human Security Approach are part and parcel of the required nurturing of leadership skills in all sectors. In more general terms, these soft skills are described in Complexity Leadership Theory (CLT) required in changing 'glocal' societies, described as Society Complex Adaptive Systems (SCAS) (Nooteboom and Teisman 2019).

## 4. Towards Trust-based Global Governance: Top-Down Perspective

Bottom–up efforts require demand-driven support and facilitation from the global system. In the current global political – economic system many projects aimed at enhancing landscape restoration or human security are isolated and scattered, while losing an exceptionally high level of energy and investment, because of non-alignment and lack of support from the national and international level, as well as the private sector.

If through the Landscape Approach - *an ecosystem-centered approach*, which includes the economy within a specific physical territory -, and through the Human Security Approach - *a people- centered approach* -, local communities and local producers in the Sahel are to be able to build productive and sustainable livelihoods, then local communities need a legitimate place at the negotiation table in the multi-stakeholder initiatives. The government is to facilitate, rather than to lead, participation of civil actors and their negotiations with the private sector. The government is to set simultaneously the boundaries in view of safeguarding the integrity of Earth's life-supporting systems and a life of dignity and opportunity for everyone. Business and investors need to act responsibly and include upfront the social and ecological costs of their enterprise in their business case.

This is a revolutionary agenda, which leads to the following equation, that can serve as a global Theory of Change:

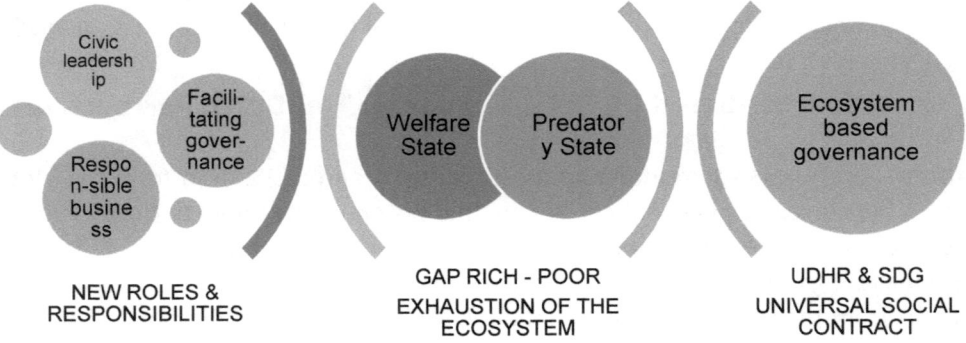

*Figure 4: Theory of Change towards a Universal Social Contract*

In this equation there are no 'Unknowns'. The relations between the elements in this equation need to be explored. The central part of the equation represents the current state-of-the-art: in both the industrial and non-industrial countries the National Social Contract is under pressure.

The Welfare State as known in Western Europe is under pressure, because of state's role to facilitate economic growth and its monopoly on redistribution of wealth. Economic growth does not trickle down (Alonso 2015) and even in 'rich' countries with 'strong governance structures' the end of the capacity for redistribution seems in sight.

In non-industrial countries such as in Mali, more particularly the Inner-Niger Delta, conflict over access to natural resources, hence over governance structures is enduring, while metals and minerals seems to serve more external than internal interests. In these contexts the controlling institutions, like the parliament, seem to be never up the task of counterbalancing the power of ruling elites. This is referred to as 'weak governance'.

In its extreme form this phenomenon is described as the Predatory State. Predatory rule can be regarded as the opposite of 'developmental', 'accountable', or 'responsive' forms of rule. To give some features of this – extreme - model: (1) Predatory leadership accumulate and deploy a high degree of concentrated political power and economic discretion. (2) Loyalty to predatory rulers is seldom based on either tradition or ideology, but on fear and prospects of rewards. (3) As well as being institutionally and politically degraded, predatory states are economically degraded by their regimes. Significant amounts of otherwise investable wealth tend to be extracted, and little is returned to the populace by way of investment in public goods. (4) However, predatory regimes are seldom 'purely' predatory, but are generally more of less predatory in practice. (5) 'Predatory' rulers, states and regimes are not new, and have been identified across history, though in modern era they have tended to be found in post-colonial contexts (Bavister-Gould 2011, 2).

'Weak governance' or 'bad governance' is often seen as one of the 'root causes' of instability and conflict. But is not the quest of industrial countries for cheap raw materials and cheap labour in the global market, for high and short-term return on investment without taking into account the social and ecological footprint, in combination with the diplomatic respect for national sovereignty, that fuel the predatory features of leadership to emerge in resource rich non-industrial countries?

The current prevailing view is that natural resources, including raw materials, are the most robust source of wealth for developing countries to compete in international economic markets. Yet, local communities are not provided with a robust mandate to manage local natural resources, local ecosystems sustainably and build a livelihood. Starting from these premises, what is the Theory of Change towards sustainable development, stability and peace? European and African states for example seem to keep each other in a 'catch 22', the paradox from which in this case states cannot escape because of contradictory rules, inherent to the shared paradigm defined by both National Sovereignty and the objective of. Economic Growth.

## 5. Discussion

The predominant rationale of profit-maximization is currently facilitated by the State. This has led to the legitimation of outsourcing of the social and environmental costs of business to society, preferably outside the State territory. Diplomatic support for access to cheap raw materials and cheap labor, so that in the industrial homeland high level jobs can be maintained and large profit ranges can be made, assures the financial foundation of the welfare state. It is not possible that all States on this globe are successful in this game.

What if we could imagine the globe as a household (Raworth 2018, 57) and start to think through how we can live up to a Universal Social Contract? What if we start building towards the alignment of all institutions that govern our daily life, from the local to the national and the global level? What if the basic territorial entity to start from is an ecosystem where people depend upon, rather than the national territory, which is an historical outcome of interstate wars and colonisation? What if all policies are human needs based and geared towards Freedom as Development (Sen 1999)?

For Jean Jacques Rousseau the State was a new form of social organisation to assure and guarantee rights, liberties, freedom and equality (Laskar 2013). This will remain the most crucial role of the State. However, today the State has the obligation to play this role in a globalized, interdependent world, where the social foundations are jeopardized and the ecological ceiling has become visible. If ecosystems, including the expanding cities that depend on them, will become the centerpieces of social organization and environmental management, then the role of the State is to shift from an orchestrating role over its territory to a facilitating role, serving multiple ecosystems within or transcending its territory. A common focus on how to live up to a Universal Social Contract provokes fundamental discussions on governance in a globalized world. The outcomes of these discussions, time and place specific, will provide a pathway for the emergence of the Economy for the Common Good.

## 6. References

Advisory Council on International Affairs (2016) *The Dutch Diamond Dynamic, Doing Business in the Context of the New Sustainable Development Goals*. No. 99, January 2016.

Barbut, M. & Alexander S. (2015) *Land degradation as a security threat amplifier: the new global frontline*, UNCCD.

Bavister – Gould, A. (2011) *Predatory Leaderships, Predatory Rule and Predatory States*. Concept Paper, 01, Developmental Leadership Program (DLP), Sept. 2011, University of Birmingham, La Trobe University, Australian Aid.

Boele Van Hensbroek, P. (1998) *African Political Philosophy, 1860-1995. An inquiry into three families of discourse.* PhD dissertation, Centre for Development Studies, University of Groningen.

Britannica (2018) Retrieved December 30, 2019 from https://www.britannica.com/science/ecosystem

CGIAR, Retrieved December 20, 2019 from http://drylandsystems.cgiar.org/regions/west-african-sahel-and-dry-savannas

ECGPW-2019 (2019) Call for Papers. International Conference Economy for the Common Good. *A Common Standard for a Pluralist World?* November 28-30, Bremen.

Felber, Ch. (2017) *Ware winst. Gemene-Goed-Economie als wegwijzer.* Utrecht: Uitgeverij Jan van Arkel.

Ferwerda, W. H. (2015) 4 returns, 3 zones, 20 years: a systemic and practical approach to scale up landscape restoration by businesses and investors to create a restoration industry. In Chabay, I., C.M. Frick C.M. & Helgeson J.F. (Eds.): *Land Restoration: Reclaiming Landscapes for a Sustainable Future.* 560 p. Elseviers Science.

Ferwerda, W.H. (2016) *4 Returns, 3 Zones, 20 Years. A Holistic Framework for Ecological Restoration by People and Business for Next Generations.* Rotterdam School of Management, Erasmus University.

Kessler, A. & Van Reemst, L. (2018) *PIP Impact Report.* Wageningen Environmental Research, Wageningen.

Koala, S. & Van Duivenbooden, N. (1999) *Joining hands to implement the CCD Convention in the desert margins of sub-Sahara Africa.* ICRISAT Report to COP3.

Laskar, M. E. (2013) Summary of Social Contract Theory by Hobbes, Locke and Rousseau. *SSRN Electronic Journal*, April 2013.

Mbow, C., Neely, C. & Dobie, P. (2015) How can an integrated landscape approach contribute to the implementation of the Sustainable Development Goals (SDGs) and advance climate-smart objectives? In Minang, P. A., van Noordwijk, M., Freeman, O.E., Mbow, C., de Leeuw, J. & Catacutan, D. (Eds.) *Climate-Smart Landscapes: Multifunctionality in Practice*, 103-117. Nairobi, Kenya: World Agroforestry Centre (ICRAF).

Mintzberg, H., Etzion D. & Mantere S. (2018 December 8) *PPPPs for Climate Change*. Blog. Retrieved January 21, 2019 from http://www.mintzberg.org/blog/pppps-for-climate-change.

Noel, S., Mukulcak, F., Stewart, N., Etter, H. (2015) *Reaping economic and environmental benefits from sustainable land management.* Report for policy and decision makers. ELD Initiative, Bonn.

Nooteboom, S. & Teisman G. (2019) Leadership and Complexity: Can Individuals Make Differences in Complex Systems? In: Elgar E. (ed.) *Handbook on Global Challenges, Governance and Complexity* (in review).

OECD (2018) *Sahel and West Africa Club* Retrieved December 21, 2019 from http://www.oecd.org/swac/aboutus/

Alonso, R. M. C. (2015). *Privileges That Deny Rights. Extreme Inequality and the Hijacking of Democracy in Latin America and the Caribbean* Oxfam International.

Quilligan, J. B. (2013) Why distinguish common goods from public goods? In: Bollier, D., S. Helfrich ,S. (Eds.), *The Wealth of the Commons. A World beyond the State and the Market.* The Commons Strategies Group, Levellers Press

Quilligan, J. B. (2015) *Great Transition Initiative. Towards Transformative Vision and Praxis*. Retrieved September 19, 2019 from https://greattransition.org/commentary/james-quilligan-common-wealth-trusts-peter-barnes.

Ravenhorst, E. Spronck and O. van Bekkum (2018) *Het Rijnlands Gebiedsarrangement*. De Coöperatieve Samenleving, RVO.

Raworth, K. (2018), *Doughnut Economics. Seven Ways to Think Like a 21st-Century Economist* London, Random House Business Books. First published in 2017.

Rijnierse, E. (2000) La démocratie dans un monde multi-cosmologique. Une exploration menée depuis l'Afrique, dans: Van Binsbergen, W., Hesseling G. et Konings P. (éds.), *Trajectoires de libération en Afrique contemporaine.* Leiden: Centre d'Etudes Africaines, Paris: Karthala, décembre 2000.

Sachs, J. D. (2012) From Millennium Development Goals to Sustainable Development Goals. Viewpoint. *Lancet*, 279: 2206-11.

Sayer, J., Sunderland, T., Ghazoul, J., Pfund, J.-L., Sheil, D., Meijaard, E. et al. (2013) *Ten principles for a landscape approach to reconciling agriculture, conservation and other competing land uses.* PNAS May 21, 2013 110 (21) 8349-8356.

Sen, A. (1999) *Development as Freedom*. New York: Alfred A. Knopf.

Van Dijk, J. W. M. (2018), quote.

Van Oosten, C., Gunarso, P., Koesoetjahjo, I. & Wiersum F. (2014) Governing Forest Landscape Restoration: Cases from Indonesia. *Forests* 2014, *5*, 1143-1162.

Van Oosten, C., Runhaar, H. & Arts, B. (2019) *Capable to govern landscape restoration? An analytical framework for the systemic identification of landscape governance capabilities based on literature and stakeholder perceptions*. (In review). Wageningen Center for Development and Innovation (CDI).

Van Schaik, L., Dinnissen, R. (2014) *Terra Incognita: land degradation as underestimated threat amplifier*. Netherlands Institute of International Relations, Clingendael.

Van Schaik, L., Kamphof, R., Sarris, S. (2018) *A Test of Endurance. Addressing migration and security risks by means of Landscape Restoration in Africa*. The Planetary Security Initiative, Clingendael Netherlands Institute of International Relations.

United Nations Environmental Program (2012) *Sahel Atlas of Changing Landscapes: Tracing trends and variations in vegetation cover and soil condition*. UNEP, Nairobi.

United Nations (2009) *Human Security in Theory and Practice. Applications of the Human Security Concept and the United Nations Trust Fund for Human Security*. United Nations Trust Fund for Human Security.

Ursu, A-E. (2018) *Under the gun. Resource conflicts and embattled traditional authorities in Central Mali*. Clingendael, Knowledge Platform for Security and the Rule of Law, CRU Report, 8-54.

# Cultivating Common Good: A Call for Transformative Science to Renew the Common Agricultural Policy (CAP)

*Anna Deparnay-Grunenberg and Bianca Llerandi*

*"Let's transform the Common Agricultural Policy into a Just Transition Fund for forestry and agriculture!"*
Anna Deparnay-Grunenberg

## 1. Introduction

This chapter calls for transformative science to catalyze the needed change in the agricultural sector. It sheds light on the current dysfunctional system of resource allocation of the CAP and its poor economic, ecological and social outcomes. While the disparity between the desired outcomes and the reality is undisputed within research, former reforms have resulted in little change of the CAP. However, there is now a window of opportunity for real change with the transitional phase of the CAP, the shock event of the Coronavirus pandemic as a magnifying glass for underlying systemic problems and the proclamation of the European Green Deal, in particular the Farm-to-Fork-Strategy. The current system is impoverishing our biodiversity, soils, health and rural socio-economic tissue. To break this downward spiral, the authors suggest allocating resources according to the common good that a farm produces. To design change, this article assigns a major role to transformative science and lays out starting points and missions for further research.

## 2. What is the CAP and what is its budget and aim?

In the aftermath of the Second World War an idea emerged in which the European Union could pool resources in order to ensure an adequate food supply, stabilize the prices and facilitate adequate pay for farmers (Chemnitz et al. 2020; Lampkin et al. 2020). The Common Agricultural Policy (CAP) of the European Union was initially designed in the late 1950s and was implemented in 1962. The aim of ensuring food supply in Europe was surpassed in 1984, which resulted in an overproduction of foods (European Commission 2020a). Nowadays, the awareness of the multifunctionality of agriculture translates into a widening of responsibilities; namely, the sustainable management of natural resources, the fight against climate change, the protection of biodiversity and the upkeep of landscapes, including forests (Lampkin et al. 2020). Around 40% of the total EU budget was dedicated to the CAP in the funding period of 2014 to 2020, which corresponded to about 60 billion euros, and thus, equaling 114 euros per EU citizen (Chemnitz et al. 2020). The CAP has two pillars: the first is funded entirely by the EU, and it mainly distributes annual direct payments. The main criterion for this pillar is based on the size of the farmland. The second pillar is co-funded by nations or regions. It was introduced with the "Agenda 2000 reform" in order to account for the multifunctionality of agriculture. It is supposed to boost rural development, organic farming and environmental actions.

## 3. What is wrong with the CAP?

Reform after reform, the CAP essentially has remained the same in its 58 years of existence (Alons 2017). During this time, the CAP has proven to be dysfunctional in many ways: Due to the area premiums, large producers received more aid from the CAP compared to small scale producers. This resulted in 80% of the aid going to merely 25% of EU farmers (Ermolieva et al. 2018). Between 2003 and 2013, one third of all farmers stopped agricultural practices, and as a result, their agricultural surfaces (and/or amount of livestock) transitioned to larger farms. Today, 3.1 % of all existing farms in the EU work over 50% of the total available European farmland (Chemnitz et al. 2020).

Whereas large-scale farms spread a loss in terms of employment, they also contribute to a reduction of the variety of cultivation systems and products (Chemnitz et al. 2020). More importantly, there is no evidence that large-scale farming achieves higher biodiversity rates or is better suited to reduce and adapt to the consequences of climate change. On the contrary, case studies have shown that in small farmland, there is not only more biodiversity (Belfrage et al. 2015), but also less use of pesticides (van der Meulen et al. 2014). The CAP structurally creates incentives for the most intensive and environmentally damaging forms of agriculture, namely that of grain and intensive livestock farming (Chemnitz et al. 2020). The continued decrease in biodiversity in the agricultural land is quite alarming, and it has far reaching negative effects. For example, the variety of farmland birds in some of the EU member states have decreased around 30% since 1990, in some even over 40% (Chemnitz et al. 2020).

Additionally, due to missing pollination through honeybees, there has been crop reduction in fruits, for instance of 65 to 88% in pears (Chemnitz et al. 2020).

Moreover, there are often no or insufficient norms to ensure environmental protection. In addition, there is little monitoring, and thus, a control deficit. This is especially true when it comes to complying environmental laws (Feindt et al. 2019). The vast environmental consequences agricultural practices present, is pinpointed by the Paris Agreement, where agriculture is one of the biggest polluting sectors in the EU's economy (Lampkin et al. 2020). In November 2019, over 3,600 scientists across Europe and beyond signed a position paper to call for action, stating the CAP is "failing with respect to biodiversity, climate, soil, land degradation as well as socio-economic challenges" (Pe'er et al. 2020).

## 4. Why is nothing happening? And what happens if nothing happens?

None of the above is new. The literature points out the inertia of the structures, the path dependency, viewing the reforms of the CAP as reactive sequencing leading to a lock-in situation. Agricultural stakeholders fight for the maintenance of direct payments based on farmland size. A study of the German Nature Conservation Association, NABU (Nischwitz et al. 2019) has shown the extensive links of agribusiness to politics and agricultural advisory committees in the German and European Parliament "thanks to its close connections to members of the Christian Democratic party (CDU/CSU) and the European People's Party (EPP): over 85% of German Christian Democrat committee members are stakeholders in the farming and agricultural sector. For example, more than half of their committee members hold a position at one of the Farmers Association's various organizational levels." The study gives examples of politicians who are found to show a "conflict of interest", i.e. that they are active in both, the field of agricultural policy and also hold key positions within the agribusiness and lobby network. NABU (Nischwitz et al. 2019) underlines: "There are allegations that many ambitious efforts to reform or adjust agricultural and environmental policy or current farming practices are being systematically obstructed, if not significantly diluted, by stakeholders. In their final outcome, negotiations on political and legal frameworks or support programs often stand in contradiction to the initial approaches, suggestions and expert recommendations, in particular". Imposing farmers to tackle climate change, biodiversity loss, plastic waste and air, soil and water pollution is often portrayed as a heavy constraint to business, that is mainly based on producing large amounts of food for the population (Hofreither 2016). Hofreither concludes that holding on to the status quo will result in enormous societal costs, endangering the climate, biodiversity and threatening the health of the people. He raises the question whether it will ever be possible to compensate such damage with monetary measures (Hofreither 2016). It becomes clear that it is time for a more visionary and more ambitious reform of the CAP. It is time to invest these large sums of money more effectively. Eurodeputy Anna Deparnay-Grunenberg, therefore, calls to transform the CAP into a Just-

Transition fund for forestry and agriculture. She is pushing to establish a system that rewards and encourages farmers that produce in line with the common good by protecting the biodiversity, air, soil and water quality, by managing resources sustainably for generations to come, by producing healthy food and by adequately valuing labor carried out in the food chain.

## 5. What does a Common Good-oriented CAP Encompass?

The idea is simple. With a remodeled CAP, farmers are rewarded for producing common good. The common good criteria are set in a matrix in form of a common good balance sheet. Ideally the definition of the common good criteria emerges in a participative process. Moreover, the criteria should be reviewed regularly, as with future challenges the European community might choose to add more criteria. Also, when higher common good standards are reached it is likely that more criteria are added.

To illustrate such a common good balance sheet, we inserted the graph (Fig. 1 *Exemplification of a Common Good-oriented distribution of CAP resources*) below. In the Common Good Balance Sheet, the vertical column shows the points of contact that the farm has with other groups of people, structures and environments, thus the stakeholders. These points of contact can be the suppliers (e.g. seed and pesticide provision etc.), the owners and the equity and financial service providers, customers and business partners and last but not least the social environment. The horizontal column shows fundamental values that the community agreed on, such as human dignity, solidarity and social justice, environmental sustainability, transparency and co-determination. Each field in the matrix itself corresponds to an array of subcategories. We exemplified that by zooming into the category *Reduction of environmental* impact. Sub-categories include contribution to good water quality, maintenance of biodiversity and soil fertility, reduction of pesticides etc. The score of the farm in percentage evaluates how well these targets are fulfilled. The EU would distribute money accordingly to the total score of the farm, which would be calculated as an average of all the scores in the respective field that a farm achieved on its respective surface. In this system it is not per se good to be a large or a small farm. And of course, if a farmer achieves good scores throughout a larger surface it will also be rewarded by considering the size of the agricultural land. The biggest change is that the size of the farmland is not the main criteria and, thus, will not be the main motivation. By following this system, farms of all sizes will be able to survive.

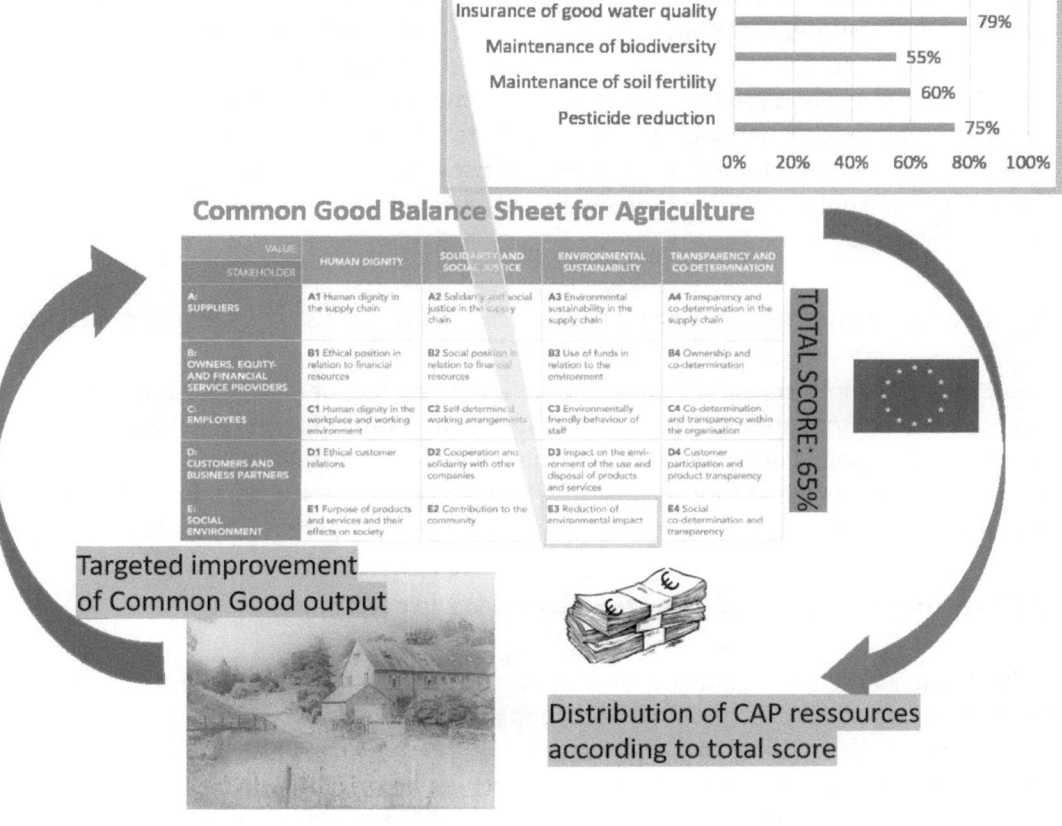

*Fig.1: Exemplification of a Common Good-oriented distribution of CAP resources (own illustration based on Knapper et al. (2020))*

With this direct link to the produced common good, large investments in the agriculture sector are justified and might even be expanded, as they include advancements in the fight against climate change, increased social cohesion, improved employment conditions and physical health due to better food quality.

The evaluation of the performance of the farm also helps the farmer to gain insights on where improvements can be made to achieve a better common good score and, thus, more money, as the arrow on the right-hand side of the graph illustrates. This will not only encourage efforts but allow for a more targeted and precise improvement. In return, this will lead to a better total common good score (as the arrow on the left-hand side illustrates) and, therefore, more financial aid from the CAP. Then again, the farmer has more financial means to invest to further improve his production. This way it becomes clear how the common good grows steadily. As the farmer receives more money the produced product becomes cheaper and more accessible to a broader part of the population and, therefore, the demand for these products also rises. A positive dynamic is launched, contrary to the current situation where organically-farmed and fair-traded foods are expensive.

## 6. How can things get moving? A window of opportunity seems to be open

The CAP is now in a transition phase, while a reform is under way and the new CAP is supposed to be implemented in 2022. Because conservative forces defending the status quo in the European Parliament still hold the majority, it currently seems difficult to reorganize the CAP and to reallocate resources. However, there are certain indicators that signal a window of opportunity for change, which we will elaborate in the following:

### 6.1 The rising awareness for climate change and the need to act

In 2019, the youth movement Fridays For Future successfully raised awareness for climate change. In September 2019, six million people demonstrated for the recognition of the environmental emergency and the need for action (Taylor et al. 2019). Leader of the movement and teenage activist Greta Thunberg was heard in the political sphere at a top decision-making level (e.g. at the COP24, the World Economic forum in Davos, in the European Parliament in Strasbourg and Brussels and in the National Assembly in Paris). With this heightened awareness for the urgency to tackle climate change, the necessity to make a change in the agriculture sector becomes evident and there is more pressure for it. Germany's Nature Conservation Association, NABU, started a campaign "My 114 Euros for…" where citizens sent emails and postcards with their wishes what their share of the CAP should be used for (NABU 2020). Pressure from society also translates into widely questioning the large budget of the CAP. Since the CAP is financed with public money, the claim for dedicating it only to public and thus common good is likely to become stronger. Money is needed everywhere and as the pressure grows the budget of the CAP might shrink. Therefore, it should also be in the best interest of agribusinesses to make changes.

## 6.2 The Coronavirus pandemic as a shock event showcasing the short comings and inherent risks of our current agricultural system

Shock events that suddenly grab public attention and lead to public pressure that is put on policy makers, have - in the past - successfully and more powerfully shaken up and changed seemingly stoic structures. In the agenda-setting literature, such events are called focusing events (Baumgartner 1998; Birkland 1998). Following the event, the attention is focused on a specific problem or set of problems, which lead to a change of the dominant topic in the public, media and political arena. The latter eventually results in higher legislative activity within the domain. A prominent example is the Fukushima Daiichi nuclear meltdown that led to a turning point in German energy policy-making, and eventually, the decision to phase out nuclear energy (Hindmarsh and Priestly 2015). Another example would be the quick implementation of a quality assurance system for the agriculture sector after the BSE crisis (i.e., mad cow disease) (Feindt et al. 2019).

### 6.2.1 The increased risk for zoonosis in intensive livestock farming

The current Coronavirus pandemic, that causes Covid-19, is a global shock event. Concerned people around the globe are changing the ways they produce, consume, work and spend their free time. This raises awareness for systemic problems, and thus, it makes people more receptive to the following arguments. For example, zoonosis (i.e, transmission of a disease from the animal to the human) can spur the interest towards agricultural policy concerns. It is crucial to highlight zoonosis here because many people are aware that the coronavirus most likely originated from animals (Hui et al. 2020). It has been shown that viruses are more likely to jump from animal to human during intensive livestock farming (Feindt et al. 2019), which is currently a major form of farming funded by the EU. In other words, the present structure of agriculture is laid out in a way to facilitate conditions for the spread of diseases. More drastically, our current agricultural practices are increasing the likelihood of a pandemic outbreak. Concerning the circumstances of livestock farming, it shall also be mentioned that with the closed boarders within Europe, public awareness for the transport of animals has risen. Newspapers have covered how animals got stuck in the heavy traffic without any food or water and of cows in pain because they could not be milked (Dietzke 2020). The situation has become drastic, in particular on the German-Polish border, where drivers spend up to 20 hours sitting in traffic jams (Götz 2020). While the CAP does not foster this, it also does not impede it, making it clear that common good and ethical concerns are not considered under the current system.

## 6.2.2 Non-resilient Food Supply Chain and Low Regional Food Security

Moreover, it has been reported that people have purchased vast amounts of goods in panic, which have resulted in empty store shelves (Balzter et al. 2020; Gassmann et al. 2020). Having experienced the fear of a collapse of the food supply chain gives us the opportunity to raise people's interest in the general resilience of our agriculture. The coronavirus crisis has exposed how heavily Germany relies on cheap unskilled labor from abroad (e.g., in Germany mainly from Poland and Romania) for their agriculture production. The fact that these workers are not allowed to travel between countries has raised concerns amongst Germans who may start to question food security and the usually reliable supply chain. While there are no shortages to be expected when it comes to potatoes or grain, as machinery has mainly replaced human labor, it is a different story when it comes to harvesting and transporting tomatoes, fruits and cucumbers (Sußebach 2020). Annelie Buntenbach, board member of the Federation of the German Trade Union (DGB), pointed out that the poor salaries, working and housing conditions are at fault. It would be possible to attract labor, also within the country, if these issues were addressed (Zeit online 2020). The article by Sußebach (2020) also underscores that so far, we have not cared for our regional food security, because it didn't seem to matter. If we cannot purchase strawberries locally, they will be imported from Spain and Italy. Clearly, the current crisis also sheds light on the societal problems in the agriculture sector and questions the detachment of the people to their local producers.

## 6.2.3 Risks, Due to Monocultural Tendencies

It is time to think of a system that is ecologically, socially and economically sustainable. As pointed out above, it is scientifically proven that the current system is not fit to adapt to the challenges of climate change, and thus not resilient enough. It shall also be noted that there is less diversity amongst crop variety in Europe (McClatchie et al. 2014). This could become problematic, if a new parasite was to emerge and attack the main type of wheat used on EU farmlands. It could result in an enormous crop loss and food shortage. A historical example is the "the Hungry Forties" in the mid-1840s in Europe, a period followed by multiple crop failures, especially that of the potato. *Phytophthera infestans*, a fungus, spread across the European continent. In Ireland, the famine took the heaviest death toll with approximately one million people. Ireland suffered so heavily since it had become overly dependent on a single variety of potato, known as the Irish Lumber (IrishCentral 2013). Nowadays there are still pests that result in major crop loss, however, contrary to the 1840s, it is mostly possible to fight the pest with pesticides. Such measures lead, however, to other undesirable affects such as pollution, death of pollinators and draw backs of pesticide regulations, which in turn further aggravate the environmental harm (Desneux et al. 2010). Furthermore, if a pest has become resilient to the pesticides, it is - as it is in the case of a virus - a question of when a cure will be found, mass produced and made available.

## 7. The Farm-to-Fork-strategy of the European Green Deal is Ineffective without a Change of the CAP

It becomes clear that farming needs to become more resilient and that reforming the CAP could facilitate this. Interestingly, the European Green Deal, in particular the Farm to Fork strategy, claims that its aim is to "tackle climate change, protect the environment and preserve biodiversity" (European Commission 2020b) without mentioning a need for change in the allocative mechanisms of the CAP. This inconsistency is now likely to come under pressure. Awareness for the climate emergency, the contribution of agriculture to climate change and more systemic thinking has opened a window of opportunity.

## 8. Define and Design Change – Use the Crisis

This window of opportunity needs to be used before it closes. Windows of opportunity present unique chances in time. A clear framing (rhetoric or storytelling), change agents, group mobilization and alliances among groups are needed (Birkland 2017). The problem must be defined "as a discrepancy between the current reality and the desired goal" (Farley et al. 2007). Policy change emerges when consensus has been reached on the appliance of policy tools to solve a problem. Change happens when "the national mood" and leading politicians perceive it as urgent and therefore are willing to act (Farley et al. 2007). Consequently, the same events can translate into different outcomes in different countries, even regions and communities, depending on the framing of the problem and the connectedness with other societal issues (Birkland 2017). For instance, the same nuclear disaster in Fukushima did not lead to a turning point in France or Sweden because it was not defined and framed as a national problem that needed to be acted upon (Hindmarsh and Priestly 2015).

Schattschneider famously stated, "the definition of the alternatives is the supreme instrument of power" (Schattschneider 1960/1975). Birkland (2017) stresses that clearly defining alternative solutions is key to gain the attention of the public and decision makers.

Consequently, the top priority in the transition phase of the CAP is the definition of viable alternative solutions. In order to move society to change their minds and to shift majorities on this very issue, the alternative solution needs to be ready to be implemented and allow for a comparison of prospect outcomes of the new system versus the old one.

A pledge for transformative science to catalyze change in the CAP and to save our livelihoods

To achieve this, we need transformative science. This concept assigns a different role to science "which goes beyond observing and analyzing societal transformations, but rather takes an active role in initiating and catalyzing change processes" (Schneidewind et al. 2016).

While the idea to apply criteria of the production of common good is appealing, it may be too vague, and thus, will not result in change. It shall also be noted that there are many similar approaches and certification systems that merely coexist (e.g. ISO 14.001:2015 Environmental Management Systems, Knowledge-Based Development from the Commons Theory etc.). Furthermore, there are scattered initiatives and processes to apply criteria of common good to companies but also to landscape management in the form of forestry and even agriculture: In the German state of Baden-Württemberg, the forest managing authority (Forst BW) is in the process of being evaluated according to Common Good Criteria (Winkel and Spellmann 2019). In Freiburg, an agricultural citizen share company has been founded. The principle of the latter is that citizens buy shares that are then invested in farms that produce "ecological, social and regional economic value". The company has developed its own way of calculating the worth of a farm considering the output alongside with the whole impact of the farm. Christian Hiß, the founder, claims that this way there are no more externalities (i.e. costs, that result for example from the pollution of the water and soil). Similarities can also be found within the networks of community-supported agriculture (i.e. SoLaWi in Germany, AMAP in France).

It is necessary to *bundle the existing approaches of defining and measuring common good and to make them applicable to the field of agriculture*. The lessons learned from existing projects should be made accessible. Weaknesses and strengths of the different coexisting models need to be analyzed and synthesized to allow the development of a sophisticated and widely applicable model in the new CAP. Moreover, there is a need to operationalize (i.e. make the criteria measurable) and *for tools to evaluate the performance of the farm* and thus be able to reward and sanction farms accordingly. A viable alternative must also be efficient in the sense that it cannot be too difficult, nor too time-consuming. We must keep in mind that the current system is very practical because it is easy to assess the size of the farmland with aerial photographs. Measuring the farmers impact on the common good will be a lot more challenging. This stresses the need for tools such as the Smart-Farm tool, which both reduces the effort for the farmer and helps set common good criteria that are measurable. Such tools need to be used and improved so that they can be applied to a large scale. Studies and *real-world laboratories that model a new distributive system or reproduce it in smaller case studies* can give important insights. The *consequences for society as a whole have to be explored*. For instance, there are also legal questions that need to be considered. This is especially important since some indicators might depend on the judgement of the assessor more than on empirical data. Processes to minimize arbitrary judgments and to increase acceptability among culturally diverse regions are needed. *Identifying stakeholders and designing participation processes* to find solutions will help greatly. Analyzing stakeholders' interests needs to be done by considering new groups, that have so far been ignored. These groups include locals that are affected by the environmental harm and changes in socio-economic tissue of their region due to the farmer's activity. This could also address a shortcoming of the current CAP: Its ability to learn and its' opportunities for participation have been low. This results in low adaptability to change and strong orientation on established paradigms (Feindt et al. 2019). Furthermore, an innovative participation process would crack open the structures of power within the agribusiness, and thus, take away the accentuate influence of a selected few. This will raise transparency in decisions made and simultaneously allow for more innovation and adaptability.

It shall be stressed that such a transformation of the agriculture sector needs to be accompanied by *measures to help farmers transition*. This is clearly the main challenge, since in the course of the industrialization and subsequent modernization of agriculture, farmers were gradually forced to professionalize and rather become farmland managers (Hendrickson et al. 2005) in order to increase productivity. The way the distribution of aids was set up also contributed to them specializing and investing accordingly, for instance in machinery for intensive farming (Lefebvre et al. 2015). It is difficult to transition to a more sustainable form of agriculture. Therefore, it is key to elaborate a change-making process that will take these farmers into account.

Moreover, new skill sets in the administration will be needed, and *education programs must be designed*. There is a great need for more expertise and wholistic knowledge on agriculture. For the assessment of the farms and the monitoring process, new jobs would need to be created. Finally, there is a *need for estimations of the intended investment for the transition to a CAP*, that is based on the common good. While we are unable to name any sum here, it is obvious that a massive restructuring of the sector is inevitably connected to massive investment. Such investment is justified, given that currently we are paying immense sums for the demonstrable destruction of our common good and our livelihoods. Consequently, transformative science is, therefore, urgently needed to shape and catalyze change in the European agriculture sector.

## 9. References

Alons,G. (2017). Environmental policy integration in the EU's common agricultural policy: greening or greenwashing?. *Journal of European Public Policy,* 24(11), 1604–1622.

Balzter, S., Bernau, P., Scherff, D. (2020). Die Angst vor der Knappheit. Frankfurter Allgemeine Zeitung. https://www.faz.net/aktuell/wirtschaft/corona-hamsterkaeufe-die-angst-vor-der-knappheit-16690499.html. Accessed 30 March 2020.

Baumgartner, F. R. (1998). After Disaster: Agenda Setting, Public Policy, and Focusing Events. *Political Science Quarterly*, 113(3), 516+. Accessed 20 March 2020.

Belfrage, K., Björklund, J., Salomonsson, L. (2015). Effects of Farm Size and On-Farm Landscape Heterogeneity on Biodiversity—Case Study of Twelve Farms in a Swedish Landscape. *Agroecology and Sustainable Food Systems,* 39(2), 170–188.

Birkland, T. A. (2017). Agenda setting in public policy. In *Handbook of public policy analysis* (pp. 89-104). Routledge.

Birkland, T. A. (1998). Focusing events, mobilization, and agenda setting. *Journal of public policy*, 18(1), 53-74.

Chemnitz, C., Rehmer, C. (2020). Agrar-Atlas 2019 (3rd ed.). Heinrich Böll Stiftung, Bund für Umwelt und Naturschutz Deutschland, Le Monde Diplomatique. https://www.boell.de/sites/default/files/2020-02/agraratlas2019_III_web.pdf?dimension1=ds_agraratlas_2019. Accessed 26 March 2007.

Ermolieva, T., Boere, E., Biewald, A., Havlik, P., Mosnier, A., Leclere, D., Valin, H., Frank, S., Obersteiner, M., Ermoliev, Y. (2018). Addressing climate change adaptation with a stochastic integrated assessment model: Analysis of common agricultural policy measures. Financial Statistical Journal, 1, 1-13.

European Commission (2020a). Die Gemeinsame Agrarpolitik auf einen Blick. https://ec.europa.eu/info/food-farming-fisheries/key-policies/common-agricultural-policy/cap-glance_de#evaluationofthecap. Accessed 30 March 2020.

European Commission (2020b). Farm to Fork strategy for sustainable food. https://ec.europa.eu/food/farm2fork_en. Accessed 30 March 2020.

Desneux, N., Wajnberg, E., Wyckhuys, K. A., Burgio, G., Arpaia, S., Narváez-Vasquez, C. A., ... & Pizzol, J. (2010). Biological invasion of European tomato crops by Tuta absoluta: ecology, geographic expansion and prospects for biological control. *Journal of pest science*, 83(3), 197-215.

Dietzke, A. (2020). „Höllenfahrten" in Zeiten von Corona. Der Tagesspiegel. https://www.tagesspiegel.de/gesellschaft/gegen-tiertransporte-hoellenfahrten-in-zeiten-von-corona/25664432.html. Accessed 30 March 2020.

Farley, J., Baker, D., Batker, D., Koliba, C., Matteson, R., Mills, R., & Pittman, J. (2007). Opening the policy window for ecological economics: Katrina as a focusing event. *Ecological Economics*, 63(2-3), 344-354.

Feindt, P. H., Krämer, C., Früh-Müller, A., Heißenhuber, A., Pahl-Wostl, C., Purnhagen, K. P., et al. (2019). *Ein neuer Gesellschaftsvertrag für eine nachhaltige Landwirtschaft*. Berlin, Heidelberg: Springer Berlin Heidelberg.

Gassmann, M., Dierig, C. (2020). Bei Milch, Zucker und Mehl droht ein Pipeline-Effekt. Welt. https://www.welt.de/wirtschaft/article206515573/Coronavirus-Lebensmittelindustrie-fuerchtet-den-Pipeline-Effekt.html. Accessed 30 March 2020.

Götz, S. (2020). Ausgeliefert. Zeit Online. https://www.zeit.de/mobilitaet/2020-03/coronavirus-auswirkungen-logistikbranche-lieferengpaesse-grenzkontrolle-quarantaene. Accessed 30 March 2020.

Hendrickson, M. K., James, H. S. (2005). The ethics of constrained choice: How the industrialization of agriculture impacts farming and farmer behavior. *Journal of Agricultural and Environmental Ethics*, 18(3), 269-291.

Hindmarsh, R., Priestley, R. (2016): *The Fukushima Effect: A New Geopolitical Terrain*. New York: Routledge.

Hindmarsh, R., & Priestley, R. (2015). The Fukushima Effect: Traversing a New Geopolitical Terrain. In *The Fukushima Effect* (pp. 21-42). Routledge.

Hofreither, M. F. (2016). Dimensionen agrarpolitischer Legitimität. Institut für nachhaltige Wirtschaftsentwicklung. https://wpr.boku.ac.at/wpr_dp/DP-60-2016.pdf. Accessed 27 March 2020.

Hui, D. S., I Azhar, E., Madani, T. A., Ntoumi, F., Kock, R., Dar, O., ... & Zumla, A. (2020). The continuing 2019-nCoV epidemic threat of novel coronaviruses to global health—The latest 2019 novel coronavirus outbreak in Wuhan, China. *International Journal of Infectious Diseases*, 91, 264-266.

IrishCentral (2013). Great Famine potato makes comeback after 170 years. IrishCentral. https://www.irishcentral.com/news/great-famine-potato-makes-a-comeback-after-170-years-194635321-237569191. Accessed 27 March 2020.

Knapper, B., Olazabal, P., Jotter, M. (2020). Common Good Balance Sheet. *International Federation for the Economy for the Common Good e.V. https://www.ecogood.org/en/our-work/common-good-balance-sheet/. Accessed 30 March 2020.*

Lampkin, N., Stolze, M., Meredith, S., de Porras, M., Haller, L., Mészáros, D. (2020). Using Eco-schemes in the new Cap: A guide for managing authorities. IFOAM EU, FIBL and IEEP. https://www.ifoam-eu.org/sites/default/files/ifoam-eco-schemes-web.pdf. Accessed 27 March 2020.

Lefebvre, M., Gomez y Paloma, S., & Viaggi, D. (2015) EU farmers' intentions to invest in 2014-2020: complementarity between asset classes. *International Association of Agricultural Economists,* DOI: 10.22004/ag.econ.212037

McClatchie, M., Bogaard, A., Colledge, S., Whitehouse, N. J., Schulting, R. J., Barratt, P., McLaughlin, T. R. (2014). Neolithic farming in north-western Europe: archaeobotanical evidence from Ireland. *Journal of Archaeological Science,* 51, 206–215.

NABU (2020). „Meine 114 Euro für…" NABU Naturschutzbund Deutschland e.V. https://www.nabu.de/natur-und-landschaft/landnutzung/landwirtschaft/agrarpolitik/eu-agrarreform/25395.html. Accessed 30 March 2020.

Nischwitz, G., et al. (2019). Verflechtungen und Interessen des Deutschen Bauernverbandes (DBV). NABU & Institut Arbeit und Wirtschaft. https://www.nabu.de/imperia/md/content/nabude/landwirtschaft/agrarreform/190429-studie-agrarlobby-iaw.pdf. Accessed 27 March 2020.

Pe'er, G., Bonn, A., Bruelheide, H., Dieker, P., Eisenhauer, N., Feindt, P. H., Hagedorn, G., Hansjürgens, B., Herzon, I., Lomba, A., Marquard, E., Moreira, F., Nitsch, H., Oppermann, R.,

Perino, A., Röder, N., Schleyer, C., Schindler, S., Wolf, C., Zinngrebe, Y., Lakner, S. (2020) Action needed for the EU Common Agricultural Policy to address sustainability challenges. *People and Nature*, https://besjournals.onlinelibrary.wiley.com/doi/full/10.1002/pan3.10080

Schattschneider, E.E. (1960/1975). The Semisovereign People. Hinsdale, IL: The Dryden Press.
Schneidewind, U., Singer-Brodowski, M., Augenstein, K., Stelzer, F. (2016) Pledge for a Transformative Science - A Conceptual Framework. Wuppertal Paper, 191. *Wuppertal Institute for Climate, Environment and Energy,* DOI: 10.13140/RG.2.1.4084.1208

Sußebach, H. (2020). Die Wette seines Lebens. Zeit online. https://www.zeit.de/gesellschaft/zeitgeschehen/2020-03/landwirtschaft-coronavirus-coronakrise-felder-anbau-erntehelfer-saison-erdbeeren. Accessed 21 March 2020.

Taylor, M., Watts, J., Bartlett, J. (2019). Climate crisis: 6 million people join latest wave of global protests. The Guardian. https://www.theguardian.com/environment/2019/sep/27/climate-crisis-6-million-people-joinlatest-wave-of-worldwide-protests. Accessed 09 October 2019.

van der Meulen, H. A. B., Dolman, M. A., Jager, J. H., Venema, G. S. (2014). The impact of farm size on sustainability of dutch dairy farms. *International Journal of Agricultural Management*, *3*(2), 119-123.

Winkel, G., Spellmann, H. (2019). Naturschutz im Landeswald: Konzepte, Umsetzung und Perspektiven. Bundesamt für Naturschutz. https://efi.int/sites/default/files/files/publication-bank/2019/Winkel_Spellmann_Naturschutz_im_Landeswald_BfN-Skripten_542.pdf. Accessed 30 March 2020.

Zeit online (2020). Julia Klöckner will Arbeitslose und Flüchtlinge auf Felder schicken. Zeit online. https://www.zeit.de/politik/deutschland/2020-03/erntehelfer-deutschland-coronavirus-landwirtschaft-julia-kloeckner-arbeitslose-gefluechtete. Accessed 21 March 2020.

# The Common Good's Approach to Sustainability in Higher Education

*Tim Goydke*

## 1. Introduction

Following the global financial crisis of 2007/08, management education, especially on MBA level, has been increasingly criticized for its likely contribution to the crisis by focusing too much on profit and economic growth, leaving aside issues of growing importance, like social justice, climate change, equality, etc. (e.g. James, 2009). As a result, a growing number of business schools around the world started to incorporate courses on "Corporate Social Responsibility" (CSR) and business ethics, but the topics were not embedded in all programs in the same depth and rigor and, more significantly, only a limited number of institution have adopted a more holistic sustainability approach, which also include the institutional setting. The article will first discuss the role of higher education with respect to sustainability, both in terms of its role in society as well as its own impact. Secondly, the underlying concept of the common good will be explained and, based on this, the "Economy for the Common Good" (ECG) framework will we introduced. After an introduction to the International Graduate Center (IGC) of Bremen City University of Applied Sciences as a case, the practical application of the ECG a balance sheet at the IGC will be discussed.

## 2. Literature review

### 2.1 Higher Education and Sustainability

The leadership role of Institutions of Higher Education (IHE) towards a more sustainable development (SD) of society is increasingly recognized and discussed. In the context of higher education SD refers both to the institution's impact on the social and ecological environment as well as their impact on and responsibility for the members of the institution itself, namely their students, their scientific and non-academic staff, and faculty (Albrecht, 2006). Through their core activities, i.e. research, teaching, and knowledge transfer, IHE are drivers of innovation and provide solutions for local and global problems and educate responsible citizens and future professionals. The environmental impact and the need to address environmental sustainability in IHE has been outlined in a number of articles for more than two decades and recently several studies has addressed the need to integrate sustainability issues such as climate change, water and energy management, biodiversity, food security, social inequality, etc., into higher education (e.g. Alshuwaikhat and Abubakar, 2008; Barth and Rieckmann, 2012; Faham et al., 2017; Figueiro and Rauf-flet, 2015; Lambrechts et al, 2013; Leal Filho et al., 2017; Lozano et al 2013; Richardson and Kachler 2016; Siboni et al, 2013; Sonetti et al, 2015; Verhulst and Lambrechts, 2015).

The actual involvement of the IHE sector took off in 2002, when the concept of "education for sustainable development (ESD)" was enacted at the Summit on Sustainable Develop-ment in Johannesburg and the United Nation announced a UN Decade on ESD for 2005-2014 and was further triggered by the follow-up program, the UNESCO Global Action Pro-gramme (GAP) on Education for Sustainable Development launched in 2014 at the World Conference on Education for Sustainable Development (Alonso-Almeida et al, 2015; Leal Filho et al, 2017). Many IHE have accomplished innovative management projects aiming to reduce the ecological footprint, research efforts have provided new insights into sus-tainability and environmental issues, while specialists and interdisciplinary courses were designed and incorporated in the curricula (Lambrechts et al, 2013, p. 66). Different to the corporate sector, where the broader concept of "Corporate Social Responsibility (CSR)" is widely anticipated, only a limited number of IHE have adopted a holistic ap-proach so far (Leal Filho et al, 2017).

There is also a considerable gap between theoretical and conceptual considerations and the practical implementation: In a series of reports the Global University Network for In-novation (GUNI) examined the sustainability activities of IHE and came to the conclusion that concrete actions that go beyond statements and documentation are still lacking (GUNI, 2014; 2012; 2008). In a similar way Karatzoglou (2013) concluded that literature on SD in IDE focus either on the development of conceptual frameworks for analysing the activities or on cased-based analyses of implementation aspects. Most authors agree that although there is a growing number of IHE which engage in SD activities and reporting, the overall diffusion of SD into IHE is still in its early stage (e.g. Alonso-Almeida et al, 2015; Disterheft et al, 2012; Kapitulčinová et al, 2018; Lozano et al, 2013).

SD activities in IHE can be broadly distinguished into four groups, whereas overlapping is possible. The first group comprises of institutions which define implementation models and guidelines at institution or program levels, e.g. the Campus Sustainability Assessment Framework, which developed out of an initiative by the Sierra Club to encourage univer-sities to improve sustainability on campus (Cole and Wright, 2003) or the handbook on "Sustainability Concepts for Universities" published by the Alliance of Sustainable Univer-sities in Austria (Allianz Nachhaltige Universitäten in Österreich, 2014).

The second group address SD by developing and implementing specific programs or courses. Several authors have pointed out the necessity to develop students' sustainability competencies, i.e. the skills, knowledge and personal competencies to deal with global challenges of sustainability. IHE should create teaching and learning formats that are inter- and trans-disciplinary, participative, and problem-oriented and formally integrated into the curricula, whereas extra-curricular activities could be offered additionally (e.g. Faham, 2017; Barth and Rieckmann, 2012; Wiek et al, 2011). Lambrechts et al (2013) criticized that the integration of sustainability into the curricula seldom follow a holistic approach but focus on partial aspects, which he links to the fact that education is still focused on the transmission of knowledge rather than providing students with opportunities to develop their skills, values and attitudes towards a sustainable behaviour.

The third group focuses on the development and application of assessment tools. Already in the early 2000s, first indicators and assessment and reporting tools were developed and tested (e.g. Behrens and Müller-Christ, 2005; Lozano and Peattie, 2011). With the aim of process monitoring and the identification of strength and weaknesses IHE use various instruments ranging from standardised to non-standardised measures to institution-specific instruments developed within the evaluation process of the UN Decade Education for Sustainable Development (2005-2014). Today, the most commonly used reporting systems are the Auditing Instrument for Sustainability in Higher Education (AISHE), Graphical Assessment of Sustainability in Universities (GASU), Sustainability Tool for Auditing University Curricula in Higher Education (STAUNCH®), and the STARS system (Sustainability Tracking, Assessment & Rating System), developed by the Association for the Advancement of Sustainability in Higher Education (AASHE). What most of these measures has in common and what is also their major weakness is, that they are generally self-reporting approach without an elaborate external auditing.

The fourth group aims to adopt or combine standards developed for other groups or purposes, e.g. the most widely adopted standard of the Global Reporting Initiative (GRI), social responsibility management or environmental performance evaluation standards, such as ISO 26000, ISO 14031:2013 or ISO 14063:2006, accreditation standards, such as AACSB or EQUIS (see for an overview e.g. Alonso-Almeida et al, 2015; Ceulemans et al, 2015).

## 2.2 The Common Good

The idea of the common good is as old as the Classical Civilization. In the Greek antiquity, philosophers like Aristotle (384 – 322 BC) considered the political good as the just, which in turn, served the common good.  In the 6th century the term *res communis* was introduced into Roman civil law, encompassing resources that belongs to all and could be enjoyed by everyone, i.e. air, waters, the sea (Barresi, 2012). In the 13th century, for the theologian and philosopher Thomas Aquinas the common good (*bonum commune*) aimed at the highest good, the divine order given by God, which could be only fully achieved in the hereafter but give man a reference to the eternal bliss already in the presence. In both order systems life and all economic activities must be aligned towards the common good. Based on this, the common good became a core concept in Catholic social teaching.[1]

In 1833 the British economist William Forster Lloyd published an essay in which he postulated that common resource systems, where individuals act according to their self-interest, tend to collapse due to overuse, which he coined the "Tragedy of the Commons" (Lloyd, 1833). But it was only one century later that growing concerns about population growth and environmental problems resulting from rapid industrialization led to a serious discussion of the commons. Lloyd's concept became widely known due to an article written by the American ecologist and philosopher Garrett Hardin in 1968 (Hardin, 1968).

Different to classical economic beliefs, scholars started to argue that pursuing individual self-interest may eventually lead to over-use of resources and diminishing returns. This led to a general discrediting of the concept of the common good although authors like Nobel Memorial Prize-winner Elinor Ostrom argued that individuals do not necessarily follow egoistic self-interests in a competitive way but are willing to cooperate and network to increase the overall well-being (Ostrom, 1990).

In recent years a growing number of seminal works somewhat rehabilitated the common good (e.g. Tirole, 2017). Different to the traditional division into private and public goods, current discussions around the common good suggest models that focus on shared governance, as well as societal and democratic participation, or as Wells (2018) puts it: "Unlike the public good, which suggests an antithesis to the personal sphere, the language of

---

[1] Starting with the social encyclical by Pope Leo XIII in 1891, which advocated, against the background of the working conditions of industrial workers in Europe, a position different from both laissez-faire capitalism and socialism. Also the closing document of the Second Vatican Council, *gaudium et spes*, understands the common good as "the total sum of social conditions which allow people, either as groups or as individuals, to reach their fulfilment more fully and more easily" (Paul VI., 1965).

the common good denotes a region where individual and community goods overlap" (p. 1). Thus, the concept of common goods suggests an alternative approach that goes beyond the idea of public goods. It aims to include political participation in the sense that it enables people to have a greater say in decisions that could affect their well-being. The global financial crisis in 2008 gave further impetus to the notion that the neoliberal utilitarian model has reached its limits. A number of declarations has since than addressed the need for more civil society participation on domestic and global level and the important contribution of education as a collective societal endeavour (Locatelli, 2018).

## 2.3 Higher Education and the Common Good

Based on neoliberal ideas, which asserts that private actors can provide better quality education more effectively, the marketization of education expanded rapidly since the 1980s resulting in a growing global education industry. We will not assess the rationales behind this development, but it is relatively clear that an IHE based on economic competition tend to perform like a business unit and consider students more as consumers, leading to an understanding of education as a consumable good which also put into question the purpose of education (Locatelli, 2018; McCowan, 2016). However, in 2015 the UNESCO published a report "Rethinking Education towards a Global Common Good" in which the term "common good" was proposed as a constructive alternative to "public good", the term commonly used in education. The report addressed the need for IHE to reconsider traditional approaches to education and to address the question on how education can and should contribute to the common good beyond borders (UNESCO, 2015). In a UNESCO debate on "Higher education (HE) as a common good in the Era of the Sustainable Development Goals (SDG)" in 2018 the key speaker, Simon Marginson, advocated the concept of "common good" instead of the usual economic distinctions between private and public good in higher education. Already in 2017 Marginson has raised the question of how "can higher education better contribute to human sociability?" (Marginson, 2017, n.p.). Especially the formative influence IHE has on individuals and its broad social coverage gives it an especially important role in the creation of social common goods such as tolerance, civility, respect, and capability (Marginson, 2017). Based on these considerations, a common good approach to higher education must go beyond the question whether education should be a public good, but should incorporate cultural, social and relational dimensions on different levels of reality and should aim to empower creative and inclusive approaches. Such a concept calls for new modes of direct participation based on subsidiarity, cooperation, and solidarity, placing a high emphasis on the development of awareness, responsibility, and community involvement (Locatelli, 2018).

## 2.4 The Economy for the Common Good Approach

The "Economy for the Common Good" (ECG) movement aims to link economic activity more closely with basic democratic values and social and ecological requirements. It started in 2010 with the publication of the first edition of the book "Gemeinwohl-Ökonomie" (Economy for the Common Good) by the Austrian activist and author Christian Felber (Felber, 2010) and the presentation of a first version of the common good balance sheet by a group of Austrian entrepreneurs. Since then, more than 2,000 companies, mainly small and medium-sized enterprises (SMEs), have been registered as supporters and some hundred companies have already prepared or are currently preparing an ECG balance sheet on a voluntary basis. The movement spread from the German-speaking countries to other European and Latin American countries (Heidbrink et al, 2018).

The ECG approach fundamentally differ from most CSR strategies and instruments, which normally focus on only a limited number of measures and have a narrower perspective. In contrast, the ECG approach aims to align economic activities with the overall common good. The underlying idea of the ECG, that businesses are obliged to serve the common good, is not new but has been recognized by almost all relevant economic theories. Thus, the ECG can be considered as a new approach in-line with several socio-economic and political approaches that aim to frame economic activity within ecological and social boundaries. The ECG do not aim to incorporate sustainability into the predominant rationale of profit-maximization but to embed economic activities into a broader cultural and social context and to link it with the core human values of dignity, solidarity, social justice, environmental sustainability, democracy and transparency. Whereas a number of empirical studies has already focussed on the effects of shareholder-orientation and profit-maximization on corporations and employees, investigations on the practical effects of an orientation towards the common good on a corporate level are very rare (one exception is Sanchis et al, 2018). Similarly, CSR has been subject of extensive research (e.g. Nelson, 2004; Ruggie, 2000), but only very few scientific publications take the ECG into focus so far (e.g. Heidbrink et al, 2018).

Central to the ECG balance sheet is that it broadens the focus and, instead of focussing on financial indicators alone, asks how a company or organization contributes to the implementation of the four value categories "human dignity", "solidarity and justice", "ecological sustainability" and "transparency and co-determination" (GWÖ, 2017). These categories are than linked to five stakeholder groups, resulting in a matrix of 20 topics, which are backed by a set of questions and requirements. With a scoring system of up to 1,000 points in total, the 20 subject areas are assessed by peers and/or external auditors. Institutions earn points if their performance exceeds a defined minimum standard. Additionally, points can be deducted for negative aspects, such as a lack of anti-corruption measures or violations of environmental regulations. The ECG balance sheet is constantly reviewed and further developed based on the feedback from the auditors and the audited companies and organizations. The ECG also advocates the idea that a change in the incentive structure could lead to a general paradigm shift, e.g. companies with an outstanding ECG score could in future benefit from lower taxes, easier access to grants or credits, or preference in public procurement (Heidbrink et al, 2018).

## 3. Case Study

The International Graduate Center (IGC) is part of Hochschule Bremen - City University of Applied Sciences Bremen (HSB) and is the leading institution in continuing education in Northern Germany. It is an interdisciplinary Graduate School for Management and Leadership, and has roughly 300 students, 25 staff members, and 99 full- and part-time lecturers. With 6 full-time and 3 part-time MBA and Master programs, the IGC has one of the largest range of courses of all graduate schools in Germany. All full-time courses are taught entirely in English.

HSB started its first efforts to address sustainability issues more than 10 years ago. Since 2003, HSB has participated in EMAS, the European Environmental Management and Auditing System, and was successfully re-audited in 2017 for the 14th time. In 2005, a competence center "Sustainability in Global Change" was founded as a comprehensive teaching and research network with the goal of constituting and further developing the requirements of sustainable development in the context of "global change".

At IGC, the initial idea for non-financial reporting beyond the already existing activities evolved out of a student's master thesis in 2013. The student introduced ECG to the management and employees of the IGC and the IGC General Meeting decided to implement the ECG balance sheet as the institution's non-financial reporting tool. This decision was embedded in a discussion following the global financial crisis of 2007/08 that questioned whether management education, especially on MBA level, likely contributed to the crisis by focusing too much on profit margin and growth (e.g. James, 2009). Similar to most business schools, the IGC already offered courses on CSR and business ethics prior to the crisis, but the topics were not embedded in all programs in the same depth and rigour. Thus, IGC has since started to embed CSR and ethics into all modules. As it was clear from the beginning that such an institution also has "walk the talk", the discussion was started on how the IGC itself can become more sustainable.

## 4. Discussion

The merit of the ECG matrix is that it allows a holistic view on the contribution of all relevant organisational processes towards the common good and to identify blind spots in the internal sustainability performance and fields for further improvement. The experience of the IGC showed that by intensively involving the employees in the reporting process, the team spirit can be fostered and free and open discussions across all levels can be encouraged. The ECG auditing process generally can improve democratic participation and transparency in two ways: Firstly, a bottom-up approach enables a holistic and precise analysis of the status quo and can stimulate contributions to improvement in all organizational processes. Secondly, it can increase the understanding and the willingness to actively contribute to a common sustainability strategy. And finally, the intensive employee participation during the reporting process can lead to higher acceptance on all levels of the organisation.

The ECG balance sheet can not only serve as tool for internal change processes but it can provide a way to visualize and communicate the contribution of an organization to the common good. Especially publicly funded institutions like the IGC can thereby demonstrate their contribution to their financiers and the public. In addition, the ECG can provide a platform for mutual assistance and cooperation to benefit from knowledge sharing and joint development of new approaches. The IGC finds itself in the middle of an accelerating networking process collaborating with other universities and research institutions.

The question on how intensively the IGC wants to affiliate with the ECG itself has led to a critical discussion of the ECG reporting within the university. The somehow controversial discussion eventually confirmed that the ECG report is the best way to measure IGC's sustainability efforts and for manifesting awareness of the necessity for curricula modification. The IGC has already begun to incorporate ethical aspects in teaching. Sustainability and Ethics courses have been implemented in three out of four full-time MBA programs. In a model project the curriculum of one full-time MBA program has been completely revised to integrate sustainability as an interdisciplinary topic. However, a great deal of persuasion is still needed until sustainability will be fully embedded in all programs.

The ECG auditing process also revealed a number of conceptual weaknesses. First, one of the major strength of the ECG, its broad perspective, is also one of its major weakness as some of the core values are not or hardly objectively quantifiable. This is especially true for the social factors. This is a challenge not unique to the ECG but relevant for all sustainability reporting approaches which goes beyond core indicators. The ECG team is aware of this problem and already seek solutions that give the audit process a higher degree of reliability.

Linked to this is the question on which basis the external auditing is performed, or, more precisely how the points are assigned. As clear indicators in some fields do not exist, the scoring very much depend on the individual assessment of the auditor. Of course, assessments are always biased by individual appraisal but the scope is especially large for the ECG. Moreover, the scores of all of the 20 fields of assessment has different weightings and it is not fully clear why some are weighted higher than others. At least a more detailed description or transparent weighting process seems to be advisable.

From the perspective of an IHE a considerable weakness compared to others standards developed especially for universities is that teaching and research are only indirectly addressed via the stakeholders. Nevertheless, the ECG reporting already have positive effects on teaching at the IGC as it helped to integrate business ethics and sustainability as a core component of all teaching activities and to communicate its sustainability efforts to students as well as the general public and, as a result, trigger collaboration and engagement. The experience of the ECG audit at the IGC also showed that the matrix has not fully been adapted to the realities of especially public universities. E.g. as the IGC is part of a public university, all financial services are provided by a state-owned bank and the IGC neither has influence on the operations and services nor the ability to change the bank. Moreover, as the IGC is not raising any third-party funds, which is also monitored by the ECG matrix, no positive impact on the score from ethical fund-raising could be achieved. The weak performance of the IGC in the area of internal democracy and transparency is mainly due to the restrictions in common ownership as well as the selection and legitimization of the management by employees because the legal framework under which the IGC operates does not allow it. However, recently a set of amendments has been made to tackle the specific situation of universities ("Leitfaden Hochschulen" (ECG 2015)) in the ECG reporting process and most of the challenges mentioned has been solved.

Another weak point is the lack of tools to measure the impact for IHE. So far, the ECG audit gives only insights into the degree of an institution's internal change but does not necessarily help to indicate the degree of external impact. Especially for IHE it is paramount to measure if the integration of ECG measures has any measurable impact on student's views and behaviour. Already certain ideas exist on how such an impact on students could be measured but it is not yet integrated in the ECG framework.

A major advantage of ECG is the way employees can participate in the auditing process, ensuring that all their ideas and preferences for areas in which they want their organisation to improve are recognized. A successful ECG process requires a clear commitment of the leadership of an organisation. Although a good supporting environment for the ECG auditing process exists and specially trained ECG consultants can be asked for (paid) support, it is recommended to employ a sustainability manager, at least part-time, as a considerable amount of data has to be collected and processed. Although the ECG has considerable merits it also shows some conceptual and structural weaknesses as described which should be subject to further discussion and research.

## 5. Conclusion

This chapter has studied the advantages and disadvantages of the economy for the common good (ECG) balance sheet for higher education institutions with a focus on the experiences of the International Graduate Center (IGC) at City University of Applied Sciences Bremen. Contrary to other sustainability reporting systems, the ECG requires organisations to reflect and report their contributions to the core values of human dignity, solidarity and justice, environmental sustainability, as well as transparency and co-determination. By this, a realistic picture can be drawn on how sustainable an organisation really is and where it could further improve. All in all, ECG is excellently suited to support IHE which want to work according to core societal values and to become the organizational role models they should be.

## 6. References

Albrecht, P. (2006) *Nachhaltigkeitsberichterstattung an Hochschulen - Diskussion möglicher Ansatzpunkte und ihrer Konsequenzen für die Praxis*, INFU-DISKUSSIONSBEITRÄGE 33/06 / CSM-Diskussionspapier, Lüne

Alonso-Almeida, M., Marimon, F., Casani, F. and Rodriguez-Pomeda, J. (2015) 'Diffusion of sustainability reporting in universities: current situation and future perspectives', *Journal of Cleaner Production*, 106, pp. 144-154

Alshuwaikhat, H. and Abubakar, I. (2008) 'An integrated approach to achieving campus sustainability: assessment of the current campus environmental management practices', *Journal of Cleaner Production,* 16 (2008), pp 1777-1785

Barresi, P. (2012) 'Mobilizing the Public Trust Doctrine in Support of Publicly Owned Forests as Carbon Dioxide sinks in India and in the United States', *Colorado Journal of International Environmental Law and Policy* 23(1), p 47

Barth, M. and Rieckmann, M. (2012) 'Academic staff development as a catalyst for curriculum change towards education for sustainable development: an output perspective' *Journal of Cleaner Production*, 26(1), pp 28–36

Disterheft, A., Caeiro, S., Azeiteiro, U., Leal Filho, W. (2015) 'Sustainable universities e a study of critical success factors for participatory approaches', *Journal of Cleaner Production*, 106, pp 11-21

Economy for the Common Good (ECG) (2015) *Leitfaden Hochschulen* [Handbook for Higher Education Institutions] [online]. Available at: http://balance.ecogood.org/matrix-4-1-de/leitfaeden/Leitfaden-Hochschulen-final.pdf/view (Accessed 31 August 2018)

Faham, E., Rezvanfar, A., Mohammadi, S.H.M. and Nohooji, M.R. (2017) 'Using system dynamics to develop education for sustainable development in higher education with the emphasis on the sustainability competencies of students', *Technological Forecasting & Social Change*, 123, pp. 307–326

Felber, C. (2010) *Gemeinwohl-Ökonomie - Das Wirtschaftsmodell der Zukunft*, Wien: Deuticke/Zsolnay

Figueiro, P.S. and Raufflet, E. (2015) 'Sustainability in higher education: a systematic review with focus on management education', *Journal of Cleaner Production*, 106, pp 22-33

Global University Network for Innovation (GUNI) (2008) *Higher Education in the World 3. Higher Education: New Challenges and Emerging Roles for Human and Social Development*, GUNI Series on the Social Commitment of Universities, Hampshire: Palgrave Macmillan

Global University Network for Innovation (GUNI) (2012) *Higher Education in the World 4. Higher Education's Commitment to Sustainability: from Understanding to Action*, GUNI Series on the Social Commitment of Universities, Hampshire: Palgrave Macmillan

Global University Network for Innovation (GUNI), 2014. Higher Education in the World 5 Knowledge, Engagement and Higher Education: Contributing to Social Change. In: Series: GUNI Series on the Social Commitment of Universities. Palgrave Macmillan, Hampshire.

GWÖ – Verein zur Förderung der Gemeinwohl-Ökonomie (2017) *Arbeitsbuch zur Gemeinwohlbilanz 5.0. Vollbilanz. Herausgeber: Matrix-Entwicklungsteam*. Stand: April 2017. [Online]. Available at: https://www.ecogood.org/media/filer_public/73/da/73dab961-6125-4f69-bf7a-3c8613a90739/gwoe_arbeitsbuch_5_0_vollbilanz.pdf (Accessed 31 August 2018)

Hardin, G. (1968) 'The Tragedy of the Commons', *Science*, New Series, 162(3859), pp. 1243-1248

Heidbrink, L., Kny, J., Köhne, R., Sommer, B., Stumpf, K., Welzer, H. and Wiefek, J. (2018) *Schlussbericht für das Verbundprojekt Gemeinwohl-Ökonomie im Vergleich unternehmerischer Nachhaltigkeitsstrategien (GIVUN)*. Flensburg & Kiel

James, A. (2009) 'Academies of the apocalypse?', *The Guardian International Edition* [Online], Available at: https://www.theguardian.com/education/2009/apr/07/mba-business-schools-credit-crunch (Accessed: 31 August 2018)

Kapitulčinová, D., AtKisson, A., Perdue, J. and Will, M. (2018) 'Towards integrated sustainability in higher education - Mapping the use of the Accelerator toolset in all dimensions of university practice', *Journal of Cleaner Production*, 172, pp. 4367-4382

Karatzoglou, B. (2013) 'An in-depth literature review of the evolving roles and contributions of universities to Education for Sustainable Development', *Journal of Cleaner Production*, 49, pp. 44-53

Lambrechts, W., Mulà, I., Ceulemans, K., Molderez, I. and Gaeremynck, V. (2013): 'The integration of competences for sustainable development in higher education: an analysis of bachelor programs in management', *Journal of Cleaner Production,* 48, pp. 65-73

Leal Filho, W., Wu, Y., Londero Brandli, L., Veiga Avila, L., Azeiteiro, U., Caeiro, S. and Rejane da Rosa Gama Madruga, L. (2017) 'Identifying and overcoming obstacles to the implementation of sustainable development at universities', *Journal of Integrative Environmental Sciences*, 14(1), pp. 93-108

Locatelli, R. (2018) *Education as a public and common good: Reframing the governance of education in a changing context*, UNESCO EDUCATION RESEARCH AND FORESIGHT, WORKING PAPERS 22

Lozano, R., Lukman, R., Lozano, F.J., Huisingh, D. and Lambrechts, W. (2013) 'Declarations for sustainability in higher education: becoming better leaders, through addressing the university system', *Journal of Cleaner Production*, 48, pp. 10–19

Lozano, R. and Peattie, K. (2011) 'Assessing Cardiff University's curricula contribution to SD using the STAUNCH© system', *Journal of Education for Sustainable Development,* 5(1), pp. 115-128

Lloyd, W. F. (1833) *Two Lectures on the Checks to Population, Delivered before the University of Oxford in the Michaelmas Term*, 1832.

Marginson, S. (2017) *Rediscovering the common good in higher education*, [Online], Available at: https://www.timeshighereducation.com/blog/rediscovering-common-good-higher-education (Accessed: 23 March 2019)

McCowan, T. (2016) 'Forging Radical Alternatives in Higher Education: The Case of Brazil. Other Education', *The Journal of Educational Alternatives*, 5(2), pp. 196-220

Nelson, J. (2004) *Leadership, Accountability, and Partnership: Critical Trends and Issues in Corporate Social Responsibility*, Report of the CSR Initiative Launch Event. Report No. 1. Cambridge: Corporate Social Responsibility Initiative

Ostrom, E. (1990) *Governing the Commons: The Evolution of Institutions for Collective Action*, Cambridge, UK: Cambridge University Press.

Paul VI. (1965) Pastoral Constitution on the Church in the modern world: Gaudium et spes [Online]. Available at: http://www.vatican.va/archive/hist_councils/ii_vatican_council/documents/vat-ii_const_19651207_gaudium-et-spes_en.html (Accessed: 31 August 2018)

Richardson, A. J. and Kachler, M.D. (2016) *University Sustainability Reporting: A review of the literature and development of a model. Handbook on Sustainability in Management Education* [Online]. Available at: https://scholar.uwindsor.ca/ode4epub/101 (Accessed: 16 January 2019)

Ruggie, J. (2000) 'Globalization, the Global Compact and Corporate Social Responsibility', *Transnational Associations*, 52(6), pp. 291-294

Sanchis, J. R., Campos, V., Enjarque, A. (2018) *Research Project: Analysing the Economy for the Common Good Model - Statistical Validations of its Metrics and Impacts in the Business Sphere* [Online]. Available at: https://www.ecogood.org/media/filer_public/9a/9e/9a9e3a2e-6255-450c-a116-64cf31498fc5/summary_study_on_ecg_companies_university_valencia_2018.pdf (Accessed: 20 February 2019)

Siboni, B., del Sordo, C. and Pazzi, S. (2013) 'Sustainability Reporting in State Universities: An Investigation of Italian Pioneering Practices', *International Journal of Social Ecology and Sustainable Development*, 4(2), pp. 1-15

Sonetti, G., Lombardi, P. and Chelleri, L. (2015) 'True Green and Sustainable University Campuses? Toward a Clusters Approach', *Sustainability*, 8(83), pp. 1-23

Tirole, J. (2017) *Economics for the Common Good*, Princeton: Princeton University Press

UNESCO (United Nations Educational, Scientific and Cultural Organization) (2015) *Rethinking education: Towards a global common good*, Paris: UNESCO

Verhulst, E. and Lambrechts, W. (2015) 'Fostering the incorporation of sustainable development in higher education. Lessons learned from a change management perspective', Journal of Cleaner Production, 106, pp. 189–204

Wells, C. (2018) 'For Such a Time and Place as This: Christian Higher Education for the Common Good', *Christian Higher Education*, 17, pp. 1-7

Wiek, A., Withycombe, L. and Redman, C.L. (2011) Competencies in sustainability: a reference framework for academic program development. Sustainability Science, 6(2), pp. 203–218

# Linking the Common Good Balance Sheet to the ISO 14001:2015 Environmental Management Systems

*Nathali T. Jänicke*

## 1. Introduction

Building on familiar models and concepts makes way for introducing new models and concepts. The common good balance sheet for companies is such a concept, which can link to the international environmental management system, in accordance with ISO 14001:2015. In 2017, nearly 360,000 companies worldwide were certified according to this standard, including more than 10,000 companies in Germany.

## 2. ISO 14001:2015 Environmental Management Systems

The ISO 14001:2015 international standard specifies the requirements for an environmental management system that an organization can use to enhance its environmental performance. It is a methodical instrument to consider the environmental impact of an organization and to take effective activities to eliminate or at least reduce the impact (Reimann & Janson-Mundel 2017: 1). It provides a binding framework with which an organization can protect the environment and respond appropriately to changing environmental conditions, in connection with socio-economic requirements (Teichert 2016: 37). The purpose of environmental management system is the continuous improvement of corporate environmental protection. Thus, an environmental management system supports an organization with the following goals (Reimann & Janson-Mundel 2017: 1 et seq.; Teichert 2016: 37):

- Protect the environment by preventing or reducing adverse environmental impacts
- Reduction of adverse environmental impacts on the organization
- Improve the organization's environmental performance
- Consideration of the life cycle of products
- Compliance with legal obligations

- Strengthening organizations' market position by permanently reducing resource costs and permanently improving resource efficiency

- Open dialogue with relevant interested parties

This management system is founded on the concept of the plan-do-check-act-cycle (PDCA) and involves ten elements.

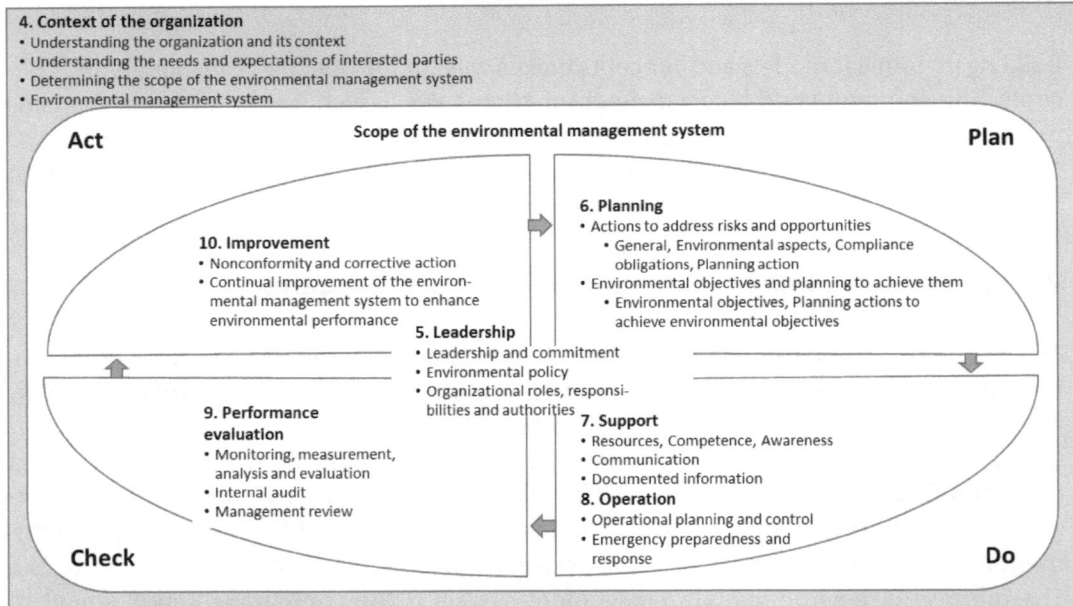

*Based on Brauweiler et al. 2015:52*

Since 1999, increasingly more organizations have been using the standard, particularly in Europe, and in the East Asian and Pacific regions. Many organizations have significantly improved their environmental performance in recent years and are constantly looking for new ideas for improvements. Perhaps one of the reasons for the decline in Europe is the lack of new ideas for improvements. A good option is to link the environmental management system with the ECG balance sheet.

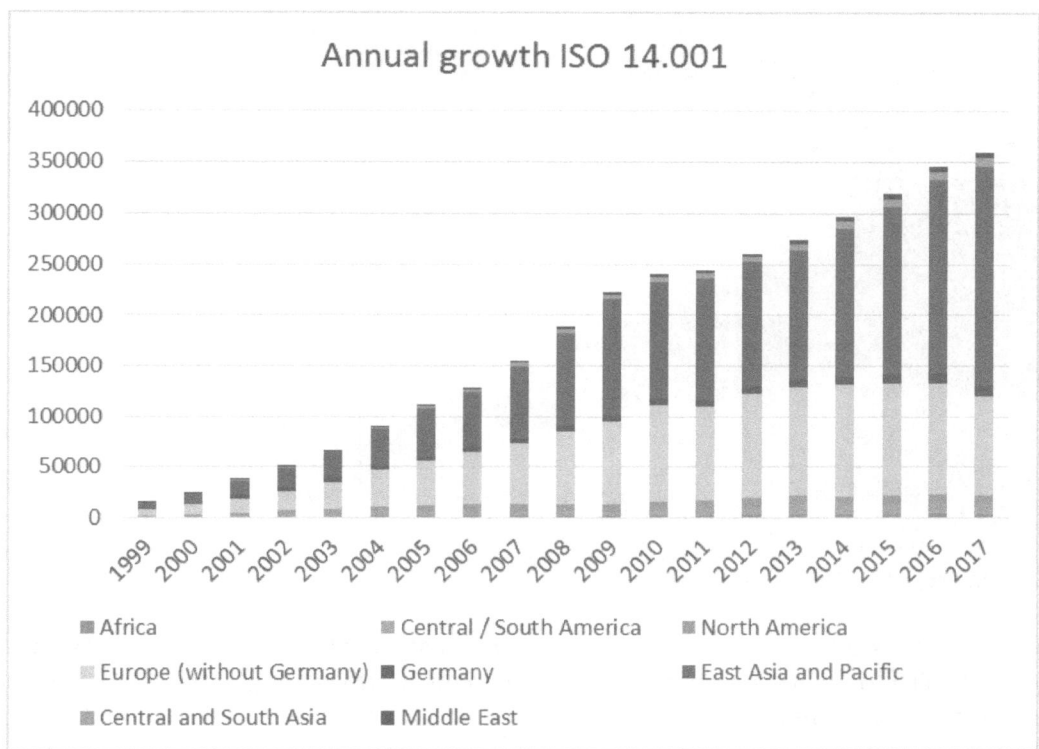

Annual growth ISO 14.001

*Based on ISO 2019*

Connecting the ECG balance sheet and the environmental management system

The following figure shows the Common Good Matrix with five stakeholder groups and, in particular, the five topics related to the value of ecological sustainability.

| VALUE / STAKEHOLDER | HUMAN DIGNITY | SOLIDARITY AND SOCIAL JUSTICE | ENVIRONMENTAL SUSTAINABILITY | TRANSPARENCY AND CO-DETERMINATION |
|---|---|---|---|---|
| **A:** SUPPLIERS | **A1** Human dignity in the supply chain | **A2** Solidarity and social justice in the supply chain | **A3** Environmental sustainability in the supply chain | **A4** Transparency and co-determination in the supply chain |
| **B:** OWNERS, EQUITY- AND FINANCIAL SERVICE PROVIDERS | **B1** Ethical position in relation to financial resources | **B2** Social position in relation to financial resources | **B3** Use of funds in relation to the environment | **B4** Ownership and co-determination |
| **C:** EMPLOYEES | **C1** Human dignity in the workplace and working environment | **C2** Self-determined working arrangements | **C3** Environmentally friendly behaviour of staff | **C4** Co-determination and transparency within the organisation |
| **D:** CUSTOMERS AND BUSINESS PARTNERS | **D1** Ethical customer relations | **D2** Cooperation and solidarity with other companies | **D3** Impact on the environment of the use and disposal of products and services | **D4** Customer participation and product transparency |
| **E:** SOCIAL ENVIRONMENT | **E1** Purpose of products and services and their effects on society | **E2** Contribution to the community | **E3** Reduction of environmental impact | **E4** Social co-determination and transparency |

Based on ecogood 2019

Both the matrix and the environmental management system use the stakeholder approach, aiming to reduce environmental impact. In the fourth chapter, ISO 14001 requires recording of the context of an organization, in particular the needs and expectations of interested parties, with an impact on environmental management system and environmental performance of the organization (Reimann & Janson-Mundel 2017: 13 et seqq.).

The interested parties include the following (Teichert 2016: 57):
- owner
- capital providers (banks, shareholders, insurance companies)
- customers
- suppliers
- competitors
- consumers
- employee
- unions
- authorities

- NGOs, especially environmental associations
- media
- neighborhood and the public

The sixth chapter of ISO 14001 identifies associated opportunities and risks and derives activities (Reimann & Janson-Mundel 2017: 35). A selection of these stakeholders is used in the ECG matrix, illustrating the connecting points of the topics of ecological sustainability with the environmental management system.

### A3 Environmental sustainability in the supply chain

*"An ECG company...*
*evaluates the life cycle and supply chain of goods and services according to any negative environmental impact they may have.*
*chooses the most environmentally friendly options when making purchases.*
*avoids as far as is feasible any goods and services with a significant impact on the environment."* (ecogood 2019: 26)

There are two criteria to consider:
A3.1 Environmental impact throughout the supply chain
A3.2 Negative aspect: disproportionate environmental impact within the supply chain

An ISO 14001 environmental management system includes the life cycle perspective, but only the parts an organization can control or influence with its activities, products and services (Teichert 2016: 85). Furthermore, the environmental management system includes suppliers as an interested party to understand their needs and expectations, and identifies risks and chances related to the environmental management system and environmental performance. The resulting activities are part of the action program to be developed. Moreover, the environmental management system includes the acquisition of raw materials, including extraction as an environmental aspect, but also only the parts an organization can control or influence with its activities, products and services.

There is a large overlap between the two concepts, especially with regard to the restriction of not being able to record the entire supply chain. If an organization with an ISO 14001 environmental management system wants to introduce the ECG balanced sheet, it starts at the advanced level: "First, measures have been put into place to reduce the environmental risk or impact associated with the purchase of goods and services. There is a commitment to reduce the use of environmentally damaging products. Initial steps have

been taken to encourage suppliers to reduce environmentally damaging activities."
(ecogood 2017: 27)

### B3 Use of funds in relation to social and environmental impacts
*"An ECG company...*
*carries out a regular assessment of ways to reduce its environmental footprint when de-*
*ciding on its investments*
*also considers potential socio-environmental effects when investing in intangible assets*
*and financial investments.*
*invests excess funds in socio-environmental projects, once the need for building up its*
*own financial reserves to ensure its future sustainable development has been met."*
*(ecogood 2017: 40)*

There are three criteria to consider:
B3.1 Environmental quality of investments
B3.2 Common Good-orientated investment
B3.3 Negative aspect: reliance on environmentally unsafe resources

An ISO 14001 environmental management system does not consider financial investments or an environmental footprint. But it includes owners, equity and financial service
providers as interested parties to understand their needs and expectations, and to identify risks and chances related to the environmental management system and environmental performance. The resulting activities are part of developing the action program. Moreover, the environmental management system includes the acquisition of design and developing facilities, operation and maintenance of facilities, organizational assets and infrastructure, as an environmental aspect (ISO 14001:2015: 54), including critical resources. Furthermore, the environmental management system includes environmental
redevelopment requirements as an internal issue (Reimann & Janson-Mundel 2017: 11),
according to the context of an organization to identify risks and chances related to the
environmental management system and its environmental performance.
There is a small overlap between the two concepts. If an organization with an ISO 14001
environmental management system wants to introduce the ECG balanced sheet, it starts
at the baseline with environmental quality of investments: "The company fully complies
with all industry, location or commercial licensing of environmental regulations."
(ecogood 2017: 41)

### C3 Environmentally friendly behaviour of staff
*"An ECG company...*

*develops environmental awareness, and promotes environmentally friendly behavior of its staff.*

*creates a framework for the implementation of projects that foster sustainable practices.*
*contributes to the implementation of key environmental measures through its organizational culture and internal processes." (ecogood 2017: 59)*

There are four criteria to consider:
C3.1 Food during work hours
C3.2 Travel to work
C3.3 Organizational culture, cultivating awareness for an environmentally-friendly approach
C3.4 Negative aspect: guidance on waste/ environmentally damaging practices

An ISO 14001 environmental management system does not consider food during work hours or travel to work, but it includes the issues as an interested party to understand their needs and expectations and to identify risks and chances related to the environmental management system and the environmental performance. The resulting activities are part of the action program to be developed. Moreover the environmental management system includes the organizational culture, cultivating awareness for an environmentally-friendly approach in the chapter seven about competences, awareness and communication (Teichert 2016: 114-124; Reimann & Janson-Mundel 2017: 78-89). If there are environmentally damaging practices, the ISO makes annual audits to reduce these practices (Teichert 2016: 159-163; Reimann & Janson-Mundel 2017: 131-146).

There is a large overlap between the two concepts. If an organization with an ISO 14001 environmental management system wants to introduce the ECG balanced sheet, it starts at the exemplary level for awareness raising programs for all employees: "There are awareness raising programmes for all employees run by the organisation, e.g. regular surveys or discussions on environmentally friendly behaviour, and innovative approaches to raising environmental awareness." (ecogood 2017: 62)

D3 Impact on the environment of the use and disposal of products and services
"An ECG company...
provides comprehensive information about the environmental life cycle of its products and services, including their use and disposal;
aims to fully understand the environmental impacts of use and disposal and to minimize these to the greatest extent possible;

offers products and services which have a less significant negative impact on the environment through their use and disposal than existing alternatives;
investigates the way in which customers use and dispose of its products and seeks to exert a moderating influence (working towards sufficiency)." (ecogood 2017: 80)

There are three criteria to consider:
D3.1 Environmental cost-benefit ratio of products and services (efficiency and consistency)
D3.2 Moderate use of products and services (sufficiency)
D3.3 Negative aspect: willful disregard of disproportionate environmental impacts

An ISO 14001 environmental management system includes customers as an interested party to understand their needs and expectations and to identify risks and chances related to the environmental management system and the environmental performance. The resulting activities are part of the action program to be developed. Furthermore, the environmental management system includes the products and services considering the life cycle perspective, but only the parts an organization can control or influence with its activities, products and services (Teichert 2016: 85). It also includes the storage, use and end-of-life treatment of products as an environmental aspect, limited to the parts an organization can control or influence with its activities, products and services. The ISO 14001 connects with the ISO 14.006:2011 guidelines for incorporating eco-design. However, there is no specific approach to moderate use of products and services in terms of sufficiency.

There is an overlap between the two concepts. If an organization with an ISO 14001 environmental management system wants to introduce the ECG balanced sheet, it starts at the advanced level for efficiency and consistency: "Comprehensive data on environmental impacts are available for the majority of the portfolio. There is a clear, comprehensible strategy and discernible measures are in place to reduce the environmental impact of the overall portfolio. Products and services largely have a less significant environmental impact than comparable alternatives." (ecogood 2017: 81) However, it starts at the baseline for sufficiency: "The company does not actively promote sufficiency, but it also does not knowingly allow disproportionate environmental impacts to be incurred. The company complies with legal requirements in communications with customers regarding the environmental impacts of its products and services and is not misleading." (ecogood 2017: 83)

### E3 Reduction of environmental impact

*"An ECG company...*

*describes the life cycle of its products and services within the company and collects and documents their environmental impact.*
*actively addresses the environmental impact of its core activities.*
*continuously reduces any negative environmental impact, and designs its procedures and processes to be resource-efficient, economical and low in harmful substances.*
*shares its knowledge and improvements within the industry with other stakeholders."*
*(ecogood 2017: 103)*

There are three criteria to consider:
E3.1 Absolute impact and management strategy
E3.2 Relative impact
E3.3 Negative aspect: infringement of environmental regulations and disproportionate environmental pollution

The spirit and purpose of an environmental management system is to reduce absolute environmental impacts. The ISO 14001 environmental management system helps to determine those aspects that have or can have a significant environmental impact and to develop actions to address its significant environmental aspects and to continually improve the suitability, adequacy and effectiveness of the environmental management system to enhance environmental performance (Reimann & Janson-Mundel 2017: 158). The environmental management system includes public authorities, for example, as an interested party to understand their needs and expectations and to identify risks and chances related to the environmental management system and the environmental performance. The resulting activities are part of the action program to be developed. It can also include comparisons with other companies in the sector or region as an external issue also to identify risks and chances related to the environmental management system and the environmental performance. Furthermore, it supports compliance with its compliance obligations. Otherwise, the organization could lose its operating license.

There is the largest overlap between the two concepts. If an organization with an ISO 14001 environmental management system wants to introduce the ECG balanced sheet, it starts at the experienced level: "The company's efforts in reducing its environmental footprint is above the industry average, and it has put clearly recognisable measures into place to improve further." (ecogood 2017: 106)

## 3. Similarities and Differences

In comparison, both concepts have the systematic continuous improvement, the use of the stakeholder approach and the reduction of environmental impacts in common.
The ISO 14001 environmental management system offers a complete management system based on the plan-do-check-act-cycle to improve the system and the environmental performance of an organization. The ECG balanced sheet, on the other hand, offers a framework for the organizational development and evaluation of business activities and the common good. It contains a guidance for evaluating contributions to the common good and is basis for creating a Common Good Report, a comprehensive account of an organization's standing in relation to the common good.

The ECG balanced sheet only focuses on five interested parties, while the ISO 14001 environmental management system allows free choice of stakeholders. The ECG balance sheet contains a holistic approach including human dignity, solidarity and social justice, environmental sustainability, transparency and co-determination. Accordingly, the scope of the ISO 14001 environmental management system is smaller and the scope of the balance sheet is larger.

## 4. Integration into the Environmental Management System

The following table shows a proposal for the integration of the ecological sustainability of the common good balance into the environmental management system of the ISO 14001.

| Interested parties | Needs and expectations | Potential risks (R) and chances (C) related to the EMS and environmental performance | Actions to address risks and opportunities |
|---|---|---|---|
| Suppliers | | R: disproportionate environmental impact within the supply chain | |
| Owners, equity and financial service providers | financial investments or an environmental footprint | R: reliance on environmentally unsafe resources | |

| | | | |
|---|---|---|---|
| Employees | food during work hours or travel to work | R: guidance on waste/ environmentally damaging practices | |
| Customers and business partners | | R: wilful disregard of disproportionate environmental impacts | |
| Social environment | | R: infringement of environmental regulations and disproportionate environmental pollution | |

*Own representation*

## 5. References

Brauweiler, J.; Zenker-Hoffmann, A.; Will, M. (2015): Umweltmanagementsysteme nach ISO 14001. Grundwissen für Praktiker, Wiesbaden: Springer-Gabler.

ecogood (2017): workbook FULL balance sheet 5.0; retrieved from https://www.ecogood.org/media/filer_public/56/e8/56e8c64e-c940-431b-8e7f-dce680bb8737/ecg_full_balance_sheet_workbook.pdf.

ecogood (2019): Common Good Matrix; retrieved from https://www.ecogood.org/en/our-work/common-good-balance-sheet/common-good-matrix/.

International Organization for Standardization (ISO) (2019): The ISO Survey; retrieved from https://www.iso.org/the-iso-survey.html.

ISO 14001:2015 (2015): Environmental management systems – Requirements with guidance for use; Berlin: Beuth.
Reimann, G. & Janson-Mundel, O. (2017): Erfolgreiches Umweltmanagement nach DIN EN

ISO 14001:2015 - Lösungen zur praktischen Umsetzung; Berlin: Beuth-Verlag.
Teichert, V. (2016): Umweltmanagement nach ISO 14001:2015 - Die Revision: Änderungen, Auswirkungen, Umsetzung; Kissing: WEKA Media.

# Process Design and Transformation towards Commoning

*Christian Stary*

## 1. Introduction

Several initiatives[2] have started the public debate on the Economy for the Common Good (ECG). Practical implementations (Viest, 2017; Camen et al., 2018) can already serve as role models for transforming business operation towards the ECG. Since the common good refers to the totality of economic activities, well-being of man and nature equals business requirements (Felber, 2014). Helfrich et al. (2015) have collected several ECG cases, revealing the variety of required domain knowledge and skills when shifting traditional business understanding and operation towards the ECG.

The ultimate resource are commons. *Commons* are neither particular objects nor resources or goods, they are social structures and processes - they represent an organization in itself. The handling of resources is of importance, but not exclusively in the focus of ECG activities. *Commoning* is the conscious and continuous work of persons as agents of action for the benefit of an ECG. Such acting agents are referred to as *commoners*. Their actions are characterized by creativity and continuous change as soon as they produce commons. Commons are not objects that stand alone, but are connected to commoners and their radius of action. Their scope of action is characterized by changing patterns of behavior in order to take the well-being of people and the environment into account in the respective economic context. If these can be captured in models and communicated, they provide insight into the current status of the development of commoning in an economically relevant field of action.

In this work, a study is reported (Hattenberger et al., 2018) aiming to uncover knowledge required for transformation and to analyze ECG operations by means of business process modeling and validation. The result should be practical guidelines on how to transform existing businesses to ECG-conform ones on an operational level. In the following we introduce the methodological approach and argue for taking an engineering perspective before exemplifying its application for digital exploration labs. The presented case allows

---

[2] https://www.ecogood.org/, https://www.nzz.ch/meinung/macrons-traum-gemeinwohl-per-gesetz-ld.1367969, https://www.manager-magazin.de/politik/deutschland/mietendeckel-angela-merkel-setzt-lieber-auf-mehr-wohnungsbau-a-1272512.html

deriving inputs for an operational transformation framework which are in line with further transformation studies provided in Füreder et al. (2018). Finally, further research is sketched in the conclusion of the contribution.

## 2. Methodological Approach

In this section procedural details for analyzing ECG approaches from an engineering perspective are provided. Benefits of studying findings from the field through the lens of Business Process Management (BPM) (Weske, 2012) with respect to designing transformation processes (Fleischmann et al., 2018) are given.

Models of commoning processes enable to represent existing practical experiences with the commoning concept and thus knowledge for creating the common good. They enable depicting commoners' practice and document operational information. When detailing ECG practice as published by Helfrich et al. (2015), we took a look in detail at the roles of the actors and their interactions and activities (Füreder et al., 2018). The cases target ensuring environmental and social sustainability, as well as cooperation in various socioeconomic fabrics. Based on a semantic content analysis, actor behavior and interactions can be represented as semantic process designs. These include:

- The *roles of each stakeholder or actor* (including technical systems) contributing to the common good, e.g., brokerage platform, service provider, homeowner, maker.

- *Activities* that set the actors in their respective roles, e.g., check availability, compare interests, check environmental impact, and handle project proposals.

- *Resources*, i.e. information, services, goods which the actors process in their respective roles or require to carry out their activities, e.g., offer of good / service, provided input, public interest balance criteria.

- *Results*, i.e. information, services, goods which the actors generate in their respective roles by performing their activities or by interaction with others, e.g., availability of housing or exchangeable goods, public interest balance.

- The *sequence* in which the actors arrange activities in their respective roles, including the events which trigger them or influence their interaction with other roles, e.g., offering a viable housing option, a good or a service after their production / generation.

These elements not only constitute process models by summarizing when and who sets which activities under which conditions and with what results, but also allow the testing of the models in the sense of executable processes and operational business simulation (Fleischmann et al., 2018).

Process models have been used to represent meaningful ECG behavior as described in each case study. They serve as point of reference as they encode ECG-conform or –relevant behavior. Then, existing domain models have been utilized to capture the current business operation in the respective domain. Using the same notation for documentation allow identifying overlaps of and gaps between existing operations and actor behaviors, and those captured from ECG operations. On the basis of identified discrepancies, transformation activities could be derived for each actor and their behavior in an ECG business operation.

The selected procedure triggered reflections on existing ECG approaches while opening up a design space for transforming existing business operations towards implementing ECG processes. Since both variants are present in the course or transformation, any change of existing structures and behavior can be kept transparent. It facilitates stepwise exploration and focused alignment of stakeholder interests before putting ECG processes to business practice.

A Sample Case: Commoning in Exploration Labs

Digital exploration labs have become common in many places in a variety of formats, e.g., makerspaces (grandgarage.eu). Besides providing space for individual digital skill development and collaborative work, they aim to actively promote engagement and knowledge sharing, including the discussion of ideas, possible constructions, and socio-technical system designs (Cress et al., 2016; Peppler et al., 2016). By exploring new technologies or new production designs, in particular for organizations collaboration between the workers and the conservation of their findings are of crucial importance (Kayler et al., 2013, Pacchi, 2017). In the following we first detail the selected ECG case before addressing the transformation of existing structures towards ECG conformance, as provided by Hattenberger et al. (2018).

## 3. Commoning in FabLab

The selected case refers to FabLab, a digital craftsmanship organization for all (fablab-hamburg.org, Lorenzen, 2015), focusing on the sharing of acquired knowledge to the general public or a specific community (Lange et al., 2016). FabLab was founded in 2011 by a group of technology-loving entrepreneurs in St. Pauli (Hamburg). It is open to any interested person, providing metal and woodworking tools such as drills, stamping and milling as well as computer-controlled machines such as laser cutters or 3D printers. Interested parties can produce everyday objects, toys, various spare parts or even prototypes on their own. As FabLab follows the principles of the international FabLab Charter formulated by FabLab founder Neil Gershenfeld in 2007, it relies on:

- *Open access to machines and tools*. With the exception of objects that could harm people, all objects may be made. Users are encouraged to share the Fab-Lab tools fairly.

- *Training and education* should help implement project ideas and learn from mentors. Furthermore, everyone should participate in the documentation as well as the guidance of other users.

- *Responsibility* - Each user is responsible for the safe and peaceful use of the tools (no manufacturing of weapons or parts of weapons), the tidying of his workplace, and operability of the FabLab (assistance in repairs of machinery and tools should give notice when problems occur).

- *Confidentiality* - Procedures and designs developed in the FabLab must remain accessible for use by other users. Apart from that, however, it is also possible to protect intellectual property rights.

- *Business* - Starting commercial activities is allowed, but they must not hinder open access to other users. In addition, everyone who contributes to their success should benefit from it.

FabLab users include both students who want to design a working model, science and engineering professionals who are keen to discover new techniques, and freelance inventors who are developing something new or old things want to repair. There are also many tech-savvy creative people who use the FabLab for the construction of prototypes or for model making.

New knowledge generated in a FabLab should be passed on to the community. There is no room in the FabLab for permanent commercial use of premises and machines. The worldwide networking of the FabLab locations enables a continuous exchange of new ideas and software. FabLab's members, in addition to paying their membership fees, are willing to share both their time and knowledge of operating and repairing machines. In addition, the members can also provide the FabLab with their own machines.

In a FabLab the following actors or roles can be distinguished:

- *Interested persons* including students, scientists, mechanical engineers, or free-lance inventors who are not yet registered with the FabLab

- *Members* interested who have successfully registered with the FabLab. They may use all provided machines of the FabLab.

- *Administrators* of the FabLab, taking care of the following activities: Registration of new members, billing of material consumption, collection of membership fees.

- *Supervisors* are FabLab employees, responsible for the training (dealing with new machines / tools) and support (assistance on request) of active members.

- *Community members* and *FabLab employees* from all networked FabLabs who share their knowledge via an online platform.

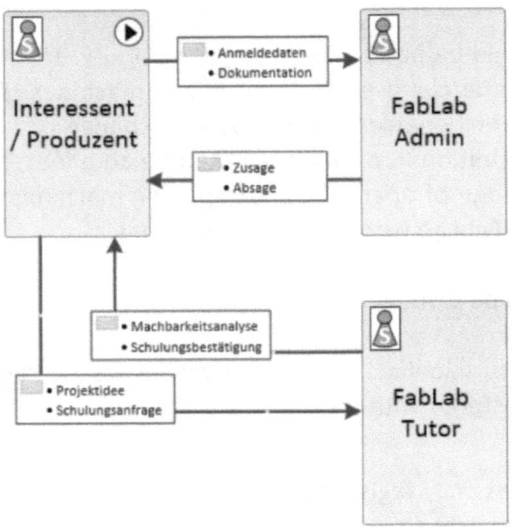

*Fig. 1 Selected FabLab roles (rectangles) and flow of interactions*

Figure 1 shows the major process roles and their interaction following the ECG concept. Several activities are essential for the operation of a FabLab. Registration is at the beginning of the value chain, handling interested people by the FabLab management, member administration, provision of machinery for the FabLab, training to use a device, use of a device, cleaning up the workplace, accounting for material consumption, and sharing community knowledge.

The procedure begins with a prospective customer registering with the FabLab. The processing of the registration request is handled here by the FabLab administration. By completing this activity, the interested person will become a member. The next activity is the payment of the membership fee by the member. The receipt and booking of the contribution is the responsibility of the FabLab administration. As soon as the membership fee has been paid, the member now has the possibility to make his own machine available in the FabLab, which can therefore also be used by other members. This activity is optional and can be done anytime and any number of times after payment of the membership fee.

Before a member is allowed to use a FabLab device, it must first undergo training. Only then a proper handling of the device can be assumed. The training of the member is carried out by a FabLab supervisor. Afterwards, the member can use the device and, at own request, take assistance from the FabLab supervisor.

Upon termination of device use, the member is responsible for clearing and cleaning the workplace. The next activity concern billing of the material consumption. Here, the FabLab administration charges the member the costs incurred for the amount of material consumed by the use of the device, which is then paid by the member.

The last and most important activity in terms of commoning is the sharing of acquired knowledge with the community. Once the workstation has been cleaned and the material costs have been paid, the member is obliged in a final step to disseminate the knowledge generated by using the device, in form of a report made available to the FabLab community via an online platform. Accordingly, from every single usage of a device machine benefits the entire FabLab community. This feature entitles the process to be an ECG one.

The case study analysis on the actors and roles as well as the relevant activities of a FabLab has been continued with the development of an executable process model in which the activities and processes in a FabLab are modeled. One of the major processes is the project specification and clearance before starting to work on a project – see also Figure 2 for an UML (www.uml.org) specification: After an Interested Party has successfully registered with the FabLab, he/she will be given the task to formulate a project idea regarding his/her project. This means that the Interested Party textually describes which project should be implemented or which activities should be carried out. This project idea in text form will be sent to the FabLab Tutor.

The FabLab Tutor now carries out a feasibility study on the project idea in order to decide whether this project idea can be implemented with the tools available in the FabLab. The feasibility study comprises a check whether the project can be implemented successfully with the available FabLab inventory. If the FabLab Tutor comes to the conclusion that the formulated project idea is not feasible to this extent, he/she formulates a report with the analysis results and sends it to the Interested Party. Thereby, the Interested Partys is informed which of the activities can be implemented in the desired manner in the FabLab and which not. This report may also contain suggestions for alternative approaches. In case of a negative analysis result, the Interested Party has the opportunity to revise the project idea or to formulate a new project idea. This will be checked again by the FabLab Tutor. This process can be repeated until the project idea is finally considered feasible. If the analysis shows that the project idea can be implemented in the FabLab, the FabLab Tutor will create a report with the positive analysis results and forward it to the interested party. The Interested Party is now entitled to use tools of the FabLab - thus he/she becomes the Producer.

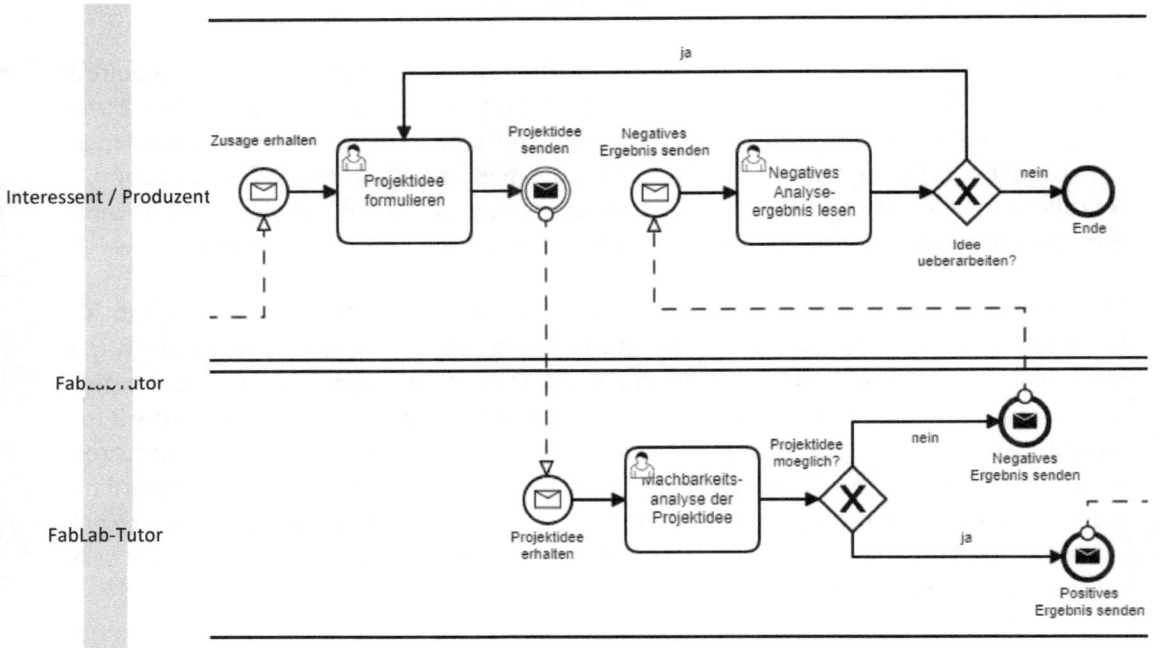

*Fig. 2. Getting started with a project in the FabLab*

Once the project has been completed, the Producer files a report and provides project-relevant content to be shared with other people via the FabLab online platform.

## 5. Traditional Exploration Labs

Traditional exploration labs, such as the JKU OpenLab (2019) are very similar organized to FabLab, however they are not designed according to ECG principles, as shown in the following. For instance, OpenLab refers to an institution in which children, adolescents and young adults (usually school classes) should gain insight into the world of science through their own actions. An OpenLab has a diverse range of simple phenomenal experiments tuned for each grade.

Similar to FabLab, a school class first signs up for a corresponding block of experiments, e.g., for a series of experiments dealing with water. However, the execution of these experiments will be accompanied by trained expert supervisors, who will present experiments and provide assistance if needed. When developing an OpenLab process, it is first necessary to identify the relevant actors and processes on the basis of the research carried out, as in the case of the FabLab process. In the course of our analysis, the actors Interested Party / Class, OpenLab-Admin, and OpenLab-Tutor were identified (see Table 1).

| Actor / Role | Description |
|---|---|
| Interested Party / Class | High school class (any grade) incl. teacher, responsible for organization |
| OpenLab-Admin | IT-administrator of OpenLab, responsible for registration |
| OpenLab-Tutor | Staff of OpenLab, responsible for school class when performing experiments |

Table 1. OpenLab actors/roles

In the course of the registration process, the role Interested Party / School Class represents the teacher responsible for the school class. In the further course of the process, however, the entire group of students including teachers is assumed here. The OpenLab Admin and the OpenLab Tutor basically correspond to their counterparts from the FabLab process. In contrast to the FabLab process, which consists of three sub processes, only two sub processes were identified for the OpenLab process (see Table 1).

| Sub process | Activities | Actor / Role |
|---|---|---|
| OpenLab registration | Check-in at OpenLab | Interested Party / School class |
| | Check of registration data | OpenLab-Admin |
| Performing experiment | Introduction | OpenLab-Tutor |
| | Demonstration | OpenLab-Tutor |
| | Experimenting | Interested Party / School class |
| | Lab cleaning | Interested Party / School class |

Table 2. OpenLab sub processes

Once the check-in of an interested party / school class has been successful, an available experiment can be started with a basic introduction by the OpenLab Tutor. After showing the students how to perform the experiment, the students are given the task of carrying out this experiment independently. Once completed, the class eventually has to clean the lab, ending the OpenLab process.

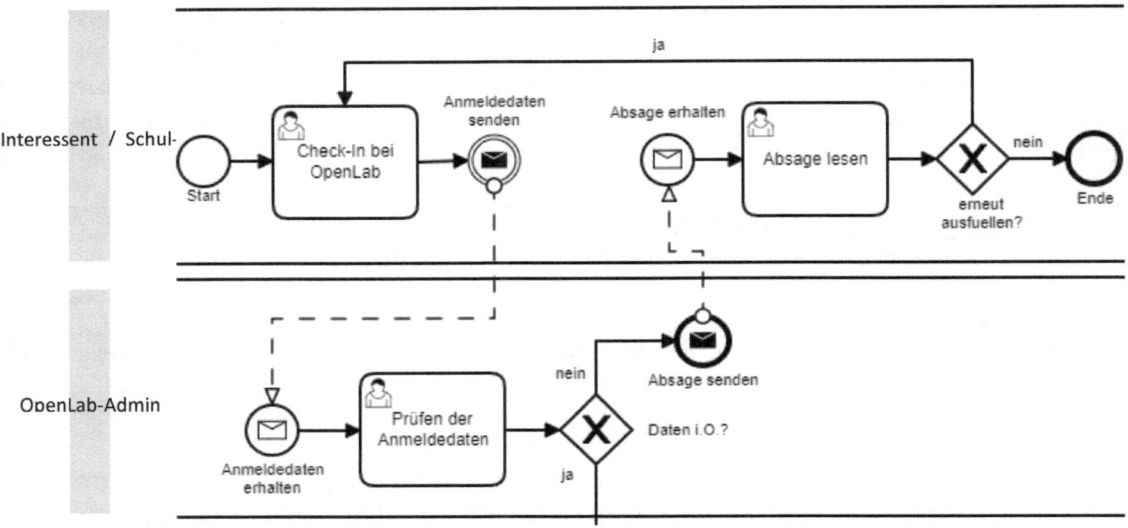

*Fig. 3 OpenLab registration*

The OpenLab process starts with the interested party (teacher) by registering the school (see Figure 3). The teacher has to enter the required credentials at check-in (name, school, desired experiment block). These credentials will be forwarded to the OpenLab admin, who will be responsible for checking correctness and completeness. If the credentials are not correct from the perspective of the OpenLab admin, then a respective message is sent to the interested party. After taking note of the message, the interested party has the opportunity to fill in the check-in form again and re-send it to the OpenLab admin. If the credentials are correct, then the sub process Experimenting in OpenLab (see Figure 4) can be started.

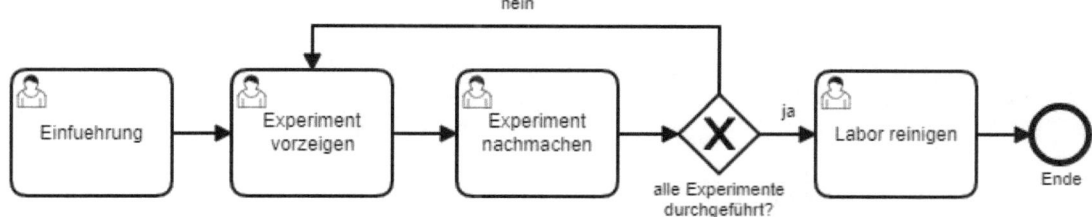

*Fig. 4 Experimenting in OpenLab*

The first activity in this sub-process is an introduction or brief briefing of the school class in the upcoming experiments and in the laboratory regulations, as well as the transmission of any safety instructions. After classroom instruction, the OpenLab Tutor continues to present the first experiment of the selected experiment block. On the basis of this, students are given the task of carrying out the experiment on their own. In a next step, the query is sent as to whether all experiments of the block have already been carried out. If this is not yet the case, then the OpenLab Tutor will present the next experiment, which in turn will be carried out self-managed by the students. This process is repeated until all experiments of the selected experimental block have been carried out. In a final step, the school class and the OpenLab tutor are responsible for properly cleaning the lab, ending the OpenLab process.

## 6. Towards an ECG OpenLab

In order to be able to realize a transformation of the OpenLab process into a commoning process, the differences between the two concepts OpenLab and FabLab needs first be identified and discussed. Based on this comparison, adjustments or enrichments of the conventional process can then be proposed.

Both processes have three actors or roles, which in principle have the same responsibilities, but in some cases take on slightly different tasks in their processes. In order to represent these differences accurately, a Subject Interaction Diagram (Fleischmann et al., 2012) was created for both processes (see Figure 5). In this diagram, the actors / roles are represented as subjects interacting through the exchange of messages. The respective process is started by the so-called initiator, i.e. in the case of FabLab the Interested Person / Producer, in the case of OpenLab the Interested Party / School Class.

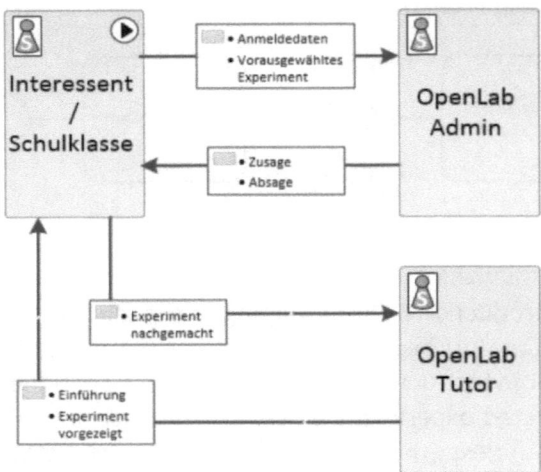

*Fig. 5 OpenLab actors/roles (rectangles) and their interactions*

The first relevant difference can already be seen by looking at the two initiators. In a Fab-Lab, every interested party has the opportunity to implement their own projects with the offered FabLab tools, whereas in OpenLab only larger groups or school classes can access them.

In the course of the registration process, comparing the two processes reveals another difference: In the FabLab, the interested party merely logs in by specifying personal data, whereas in OpenLab, in addition to the usual credentials, a predefined block of experiments needs to be selected. In the FabLab process the selection of a projects occurs after registration and after the prospective customer has formulated a project idea, which is then checked by the FabLab Tutor by means of a feasibility analysis.

The third and most important difference with regard to commoning is that in FabLab every logged in user (Interested Person / Producer) is obliged to document all activities and knowledge concerning the individual project, and provide it to the FabLab community, thus is becoming the common good. This task does not exist in OpenLab. The process ends after completing the last experiment.

In the course of this comparative analysis, several differences could be identified, which have be used to adapt the conventional process towards commoning. In Table 3, the differences in terms of access, project selection and knowledge distribution have been structured and summarized.

| | FabLab | OpenLab |
|---|---|---|
| Access | All interested persons | School classes |
| Selection of project | Only limited by available resources | Predefined experiments |
| Sharing of knowledge | FabLab community | Within the class |

*Table 3.FabLab vs. OpenLab features*

The first enrichment concerns lifting of access restrictions. In a welfare-oriented OpenLab it should be possible that not only school classes but also individuals are able to register for the implementation of their own projects. This transformation can be carried out easily by extending the check-in with an option "Check own project / experiment". The subsequent adaptation concerns the formulation of individual project ideas and their implementation, in addition to the predefined, supervised experiments. For this purpose, a new option "Description of project idea" needs to be inserted into the OpenLab check-in procedure after having chosen the option to perform an own project or experiment.

As soon as a prospective customer has decided on a project of his/her own and has formulated a project idea, it must be ensured that this project idea is also reviewed with regard to the feasibility before project implementation. For this purpose, a feasibility analysis has to be carried out by the OpenLab Tutor. It can be inserted between the sub processes "OpenLab Registration" and "Performing experiment" (see Figure 6). The OpenLab Tutor evaluates the proposal and decides whether he/she sends a rejection to the prospective customer (check-in must be carried out again) or he/she declares the project / experiment as feasible, starting the sub-process "Experimenting in OpenLab" (Figure 7).

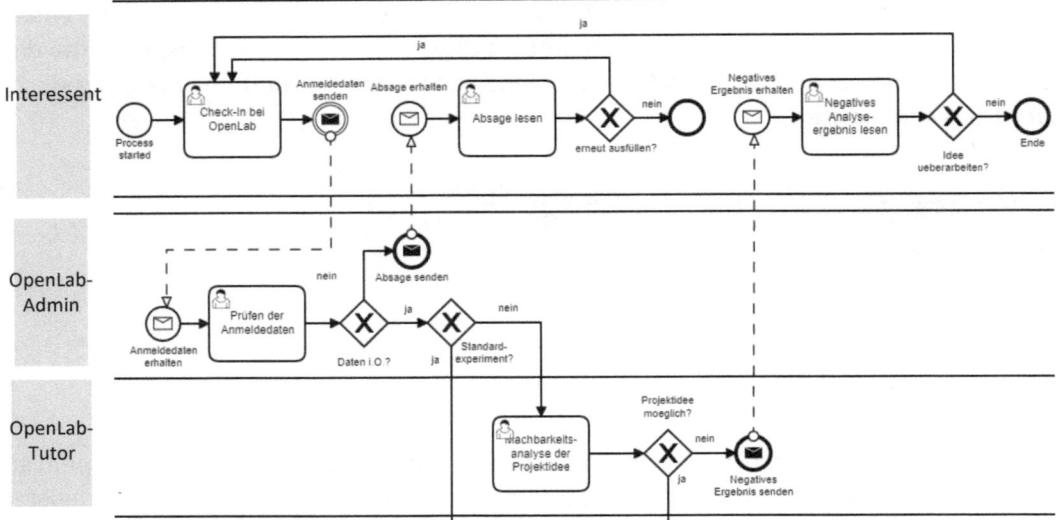

*Fig. 6 Transformed OpenLab-Registration*

The most significant changes in the process of transforming the OpenLab process model towards communing concern the experimenting process (see Figure 7). After a basic introduction or a brief introduction to the Interested Party / School Class regarding the subsequent experiment, the laboratory regulations and any safety instructions, a specific path will be entered, depending on whether an individual project / experiment or a predefined standard experiment has been chosen. In case a predefined standard experiment is performed, the original OpenLab process is run through.

In case of an individual project, the applicant receives all the utensils that he/she needs to implement the project from the OpenLab. Then, he/she carries out his desired experiment on his/her own. Upon completion the lab or workplace must be cleaned. Finally, as these are usually unique, innovative experiments, the knowledge gained hereby needs to be documented, and made available to the OpenLab community via an online platform.

In summary, the removal of access restrictions, the extension of project selection options, and the distribution of knowledge in the sense of commoning, characterizes the transformation of the OpenLab process into a process based on commoning principles. Both, the FabLab processes could be utilized to enrich OpenLab processes, leading to an inclusive ECG representation.

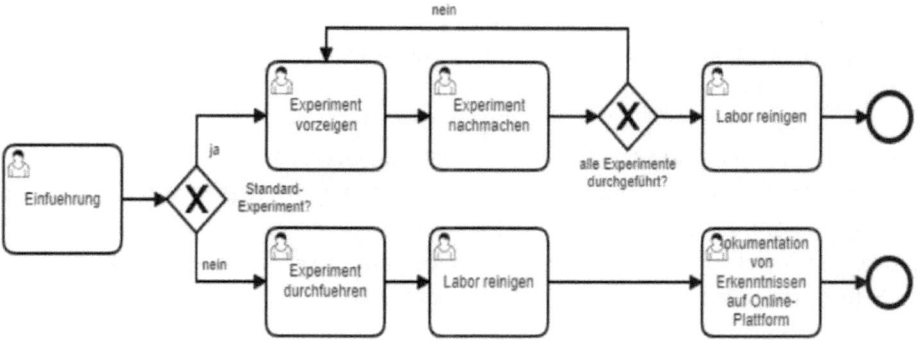

*Fig. 7 Experimenting in a transformed OpenLab*

## 7. Learnings from that Case

The modifications as part of the transformation of the OpenLab processes provide oppor-tunities for common good orientation of existing procedures. In particular, the obligation to document each innovative or project activity and, consequently, make it available to the community, represents an ECG-component of process management, since educa-tional or research institution could strive to generate knowledge as efficiently as possible and make it usable as common good.

In order to implement the adjacent commoning process, however, the scope of the mod-eling would have to be expanded in a next step, as only a simplified part of the organiza-tion has been covered in the case at hand. Further refinements of the specification of individual processes are required, in order to digitize, where appropriate, the business operation using executable process models. Executable process specifications can be val-idated, i.e. evaluated whether they represent role behavior in an accurate way, and sub-sequently run by a corresponding workflow engine, e.g., simulating newly designed or-ganizational behavior (Fleischmann et al., 2018).

## 8. Conclusions

Transformation to commoning can be based on semantic process models. These models have the capability to represent existing approaches to an ECG economy as well as adap-tation towards an ECG when still operating in traditional business modes. Organizations can at any time incorporate ECG-conform activities in their business routines, once these are grounded in the domain and modelled on a process level. In this way, semantic representations serve as baseline for transforming societal systems and as role models for all members of a community.

Even if there is a high willingness to transform processes towards creating common good, starting point of transformation should be the set of existing processes and the participation of affected stakeholders in the business operation or economic system. Functional role behavior is essential for the provision of services and production of goods, and must be technically integrated into the transformation process.

What is common in the case studies further analyzed in Füreder et al. (2018) is that the interplay of human beings, their environment, and technological developments in the common good orientation requires not only the clarification and consistent pursuit of commoning goals, but also actual role carriers. They are the ones who have to contribute through individual engagement to the creation of common goods and have to act in an informed and qualified way in complex matters. The latter is utmost importance when decision making has to be in line with legal regulations and adjusted to social settings when aiming for high stakeholder acceptance.

Therefore, business processes for the implementation of an ECG should be able to dynamically handle the diversity of stakeholder intentions and resulting behavioral patterns and procedures. Then, the involved and affected stakeholders can negotiate in what form commoning can be implemented. The reference item is always the living, dynamically changing structure of social behavior and the way stakeholders interpret and handle tasks. It concerns handling of resources, ECG services and goods, being an essential part of the network of relationships between actors (i.e. the commoners).

ECG transformation increases transparency of support and decision making processes which in turn leads to an increased number of functional roles in the interests of the common good and the commoning process. Consequently, the number of required interactions between role carriers increases. Apparently, the primacy of collective decision making in the course of commoning increases the complexity of the processes rather than simplifying the engagement of concerned stakeholders. ECG seems to come at a price, mainly due to the participatory nature of commoning processes.

# 9. References

Cress, U., Moskaliuk, J., & Jeong, H. (Eds.). (2016). *Mass collaboration and education* (Vol. 16). New York, NY: Springer.

Felber, Ch. (2014) The Common Good Economy. Deuticke, Vienna.

Fleischmann, A., Oppl, St., Schmidt, W., & Stary, Ch. (2018) Contextual digitization of processes. Change of Perspective - Design Thinking - Value-based Interaction. Springer, Cham.

Hattenberger, D., Hauser, G. (2018) FabLab: High-tech Production for all, in: Füreder et al. (2018), 137-174.

Helfrich, S., Bollier, D. & Heinrich Böll Foundation (ed.) (2015) The World of Commons. Pattern of common action. transcript, Bielefeld.

JKU Open Lab Linz, "Open Lab". https://www.openlab-jku.at/open-lab/, visited 12.11.2019.

Jürgens, K., Hoffmann, R., Schildmann, Ch. (2017) Arbeit transformieren! Denkanstöße der Kommission „Arbeit der Zukunft". Hans-Böckler-Stiftung. transcript, Bielefeld.

Kayler, M., Owens, T. & Meadows, G. (2013). Inspiring Maker Culture through Collaboration, Persistence, and Failure. In R. McBride & M. Searson (Eds.), *Proceedings of SITE 2013--Society for Information Technology & Teacher Education International Conference* (pp. 1179-1184). New Orleans, Louisiana, United States: Association for the Advancement of Computing in Education (AACE). Retrieved November 17, 2018 from https://www.learntechlib.org/primary/p/48281/

Lange, B., Domann, V., Häfele, V. (2016) Wertschöpfung in offenen Werkstätten. Eine empirische Erhebung kollaborativer Praktiken in Deutschland. Institut für ökologische Wirtschaftsforschung, 213. Jg., S. 16

Lorenzen, A. (2015). Ein FabLab für St.Pauli, in: Helfrich et al. (2015), pp. 158-161.
Muller-Camen, M., & Camen, J. (2018). Economy for the Common Good: Sonnentor. In *Progressive Business Models* (pp. 123-142). Palgrave Macmillan, Cham.

Oppl, St., Stary, Ch. (2018) Designing Digital Work - Concepts and Methods for Human-Centered Digitization. Springer Palgrave, Cham.

Peppler, K., Halverson, E., & Kafai, Y. B. (Eds.). (2016). *Makeology: Makerspaces as learning environments* (Vol. 1). Routledge, London.

Pacchi, C. (2017). Sharing economy: Makerspaces, co-working spaces, hybrid workplaces, and new social practices. In *Milan: Productions, Spatial Patterns and Urban Change. Productions, Spatial Patterns and Urban Change*, eds. Armondi, S.A., Di Vita, St. (pp. 73-83). Routledge, London.

Füreder, S., Grurl, L.M., Hattenberger, D., Hauser, G., Kremsmayr, M., Lackner, M., Lechner, R., Polt, S., Prinz, T., Stary, C. Weberndorfer, T. (2018) Commoning. Process Design and Transformation (in German) (2018), i2pm.net/books, download 4.11.2019.

Viest, O. (2017). The public interest balance as orientation frame for socially shaping action. In: Nonprofit Organizations and Sustainability (pp. 149-158). Springer Gabler, Wiesbaden.

Weske, M. (2012). *Business Process Management*. Springer, Berlin, Heidelberg.

# Religion as a Source of value-oriented Transformation

*Johannes Panhofer*

## 1. Introduction

With his so-called environmental encyclical "Laudato Si", Pope Francis has received great attention - far beyond the Catholic Church. In "care for our common home" he calls for a new kind of economy because „Such an economy kills!" (EG, No. 53) as already pointed out in his previous encyclical. It urgently needs a different way of life that overcomes the self-destructing mechanisms of the market. What could be the contribution of spiritual and religious traditions to a worldwide common welfare?

In this brief paper, I point out some encouraging aspects of religions. Knowing that this can only be a general overview, I focus on the dignity of man and creation, the meaning of the common good, the message of the encyclical "Laudato Si" from Pope Francis, guidelines from Christian Churches and examples from other religions. Finally, a short summary of the idea is presented. Even though I write from the perspective of a (Catholic) Christian, many arguments also apply for other religions, in particular for monotheistic religions.

## 2. Religions as partners in working for the common good
### 2.1 Religion: Interruption - Resistance - Vision

Corona has interrupted our everyday life. Public discussion started whether this invisible virus will completely change our lives in the long term or whether everyone wants to return to pre-Corona times as soon as possible. The answers are controversial. However, one thing is clear: Sustainable change does not seem to be an automatic process. A new development needs an offensive, resolute discussion in our society about the important values which can transform and shape our society sustainable and fair.

The Corona-lock down is a surprising parallel to what religion wants to be. The shortest definition of religion is: interruption! Religion will be an interruption of the usual everyday life course - and it does not matter whether this happens due to a stroke of fate or a freely chosen sabbatical year. In any case this break poses questions about what is important in (my) life and about what is beautiful, fulfilling, meaningful, i.e. Religions do not want to anger someone but to keep the question alive what is meaningful and essential. What makes me happy, satisfied and emotional rich? Values like human dignity, self-development, friendship and solidarity, clear nature, participation in society, fairness and transparency and so on. To discover this, daily routine sometimes needs to be interrupted. Every religion offers traditional kinds of breaks to look for personal and common essential "things": Sabbath and Sunday, Lent and Ramadan, Friday prayers and evening prayers - these are daily, weekly and yearly breaks to pause. Modern forms for this purpose are Time-out houses or pilgrimages; to fall in a burn-out is more painful but also effective.

It has to be said, that of course the break gives also the chance to thank for the bright side of life and to celebrate in community and happiness. But at the same time, in some key moments we realise that fulfilment is not complete. We are longing for greater justice, for deeper peace (especially at Christmas) and for harmony with nature. Religions and holy scriptures are full of stories and metaphors about how to reach abundant life. Therefore, religions always provoke and waken visions for a "fullness of life" (Joh 10,10) and encourage people to work for the expected good life. Taking this responsibility towards the world, man becomes the subject of his own history. Inspired by a God - among Jews, Christians and Muslims – who vehemently advocates justice, peace and the protection of creation. Therefore, we find the "golden rule" of love for others as a fundamental value in all the great religious communities.
For this reason religions stand up if conditions of injustice, the exploitation of people and nature take place. They show resistance against all kinds of dehumanisation. The sting of the Kingdom of God does not allow you to linger in the religious hammock.

### 2.2 The dignity of humans, animals and nature

But what is the point of reference for commitment? In many religions, human dignity is the starting point and the heart for all following social-ethical reflections. Many religions say that a "divine spark" lives in people and gives them their captive dignity. In Christianity, people are seen as images of God. In the biblical story of creation we read: "Then God said: Let us make people as our image, like us. ... God created man as his image; he created it as an image of God. He created them as a man and a woman" (Gen 1,26-28) and further it is written: "God saw all that he had made: It was very beautiful and very good!" (Gen 1,31) Man and all of creation should share in God's joy in all life.

According to the belief of monotheistic religions, man and woman as the image of God establishes the untouchable dignity of people. Perceiving and seeing this dignity of all creatures is the precondition for human coexistence. This applies to every human individual but also to every small and large creature. That is why God shaped each creature with its uniqueness and put "something from him-/herself" in it. And because God shared something of his being and his character with man and woman, human beings can only find fulfilment in humanity and love, in liberty and solidarity. If this orientation is abandoned - so the belief - people look for substitute satisfactions that are always only temporary and gets often inner emptiness.

Therefore, from a Christian perspective we can summarise: Orientation towards human dignity is the first point of reference for dealing with socio-ethical issues. The whole Catholic social doctrine is based on human dignity. Therefore it has a triple function: first as a basic position, then as a target point and finally as a criterion for various social, cultural and economic situations.

However, this dignity should not only be emphasised theoretically but be realised in a "dignity practice" (Sedmak, 2017, p. 16). Without such a concrete practice, the concept and content will atrophy. In other words: Christian social teaching commits to deep practice of human dignity and stands up wherever human dignity and freedom are endangered. This applies - and here Christian social teaching is in agreement with the ECG - also for the world of economics: "The Church's social doctrine holds that authentically human social relationships of friendship, solidarity and reciprocity can also be conducted within economic activity, and not only outside it or "after" it. The economic sphere is neither ethically neutral, nor inherently inhuman and opposed to society. It is part and parcel of human activity and precisely because it is human, it must be structured and governed in an ethical manner." (CV, No. 36)

With the UN Charter (1945), the "Universal Declaration of Human Rights" (1948) and following UN documents, the term "human dignity" gained political and legal power. Finally, since the eighties in view of increased environmental problems we speak also about the "dignity of nature". So, for example, the "dignity of the creature" is written down in the Swiss Federal Constitution of 1992.

### 2.3 Religions are engaged for the common good

The term common good is frequently used but its definition is far from clear. Even the state does not specify the common good as a fixed quantity. This is the case because the concept of the idea is in permanent process. The concept of the common good is the product of multifarious communication processes. It is "the procedural result of the activities of a multitude of initiatives and institutions in which citizens assume responsibility in a graded manner. Its overarching goal is the implementation of a legal and welfare order that corresponds as far as possible to justice". (Gabriel, 2017, p. 46). The religious communities are part of these democratic "players".

The Catholic Church defined the common good as follows: The common good is "the sum of those conditions of social life which allow social groups and their individual members relatively thorough and ready access to their own fulfilment. ... Every social group must take account of the needs and legitimate aspirations of other groups, and even of the general welfare of the entire human family." (GS, No. 26) Therefore, everyone has the right and duty to pursue their own interests, while at the same time being obliged to take into account the well-being and rights of others.

"Religions - the plural is appropriate here with all differences - and their ethic concepts play an indispensable role, insofar as they go beyond the social-ethical questions to the great thought experiment of creating a socially and ecologically just order, adding a religious depth dimension of their own sources."(Gabriel, 2017, p. 48) This is effective not only in the motivating and encouraging vision but also in the more or less radical relativisation of property and of economic activity. Possession is never an end in itself. Economic activity provides the necessary material resources and should be distributed fairly. Religions call for solidarity, even for a voluntary self-limitation. This does not restrict self-realisation and freedom but realises the way to humanity.

## 3. Example Pope Francis

Reading the texts of Pope Francis one could ask: Is he an undercover agent of the economy for the common good? The term "common good" is used 25 times in Pope Francis' encyclical "Laudato Si". And especially in his first encyclica "Evangelii Gaudium" he has pronounced a harsh judgement about the predominant economic system. Let us pick out some text examples, by which we can recognise how Pope Francis sees the connections between the common good and the economy.

First of all, he emphasises the overall orientation outlined above concerning human dignity: "The dignity of each human person and the pursuit of the common good are concerns which
ought to shape all economic policies." (EG, No. 203) Economic activities must always be related with the whole world: "Each meaningful economic decision made in one part of the world has repercussions everywhere else; consequently, no government can act

without regard for shared responsibility. Indeed, it is becoming increasingly difficult to find local solutions for enormous global problems which overwhelm local politics with difficulties to resolve." (EG, No. 206)

For Pope Francis those phenomena that exclude whole groups of people from participation of social life are especially important. This superfluous group stand below the exploited people, because they are still needed in the capitalist system: It is no longer simply about
exploitation and oppression but something new. Exclusion ultimately has to do with what it means to be a part of the society in which we live; those excluded are no longer society's underside or its fringes or its disenfranchised – they are no longer even a part of it. The excluded are not the ‚exploited' but the outcast, the ‚leftovers.'" (EG, No. 53) This process shows a globalised indifference and phlegm, which leads to dehumanisation: "Almost without being aware of it, we end up being incapable of feeling compassion at the outcry of the poor, weeping for other people's pain, and feeling a need to help them, as though all this were someone else's responsibility and not our own. The culture of prosperity deadens us;" (EG, No. 54).
In contrast to this widespread attitude, the Pope calls for a culture of solidarity and sharing: "Growth in justice requires more than economic growth, while presupposing such growth: it requires decisions, programs, mechanisms and processes specifically geared to a better distribution of income." (EG, No. 204).

The Pope sees very clearly that the solution for the existing inequalities cannot lie in charitable giving. This would only compensate the shortcomings of existing system failures instead of reform the whole system. The Church has to strengthen the paradigm of justice in place of demand for the paradigm of mercy (eg. donations, aid projects): "The need to resolve the structural causes of poverty cannot be delayed ... Welfare projects, which meet certain urgent needs, should be considered merely temporary responses. As long as the problems of the poor are not radically resolved by rejecting the absolute autonomy of markets and financial speculation and by attacking the structural causes of inequality, no solution will be found for the world's problems or, for that matter, to any problems. Inequality is the root of social ills." (EG, No. 202)

In chapter 2.1 of the encyclica "Evangelii Gaudium" Francis says a multiple No to the various aspects of imperial capitalism: No to an economy of exclusion, No to the new idolatry of money, No to money that rules instead of serving, No to social inequality, which leads to violence.

We find always two levels where the various statements can be allocated: personal attitude and the (injustice) structures. There are concrete persons and institutions, which build the "structures of sin" following selfish action. "It is therefore necessary to work simultaneously for the conversion of hearts and for the improvement of structures." (LC, No. 75) Insofar as structures do not change on their own, insightful, solidarity-minded people are needed who improve the fair structures in a sustainable and democratic way. So there is a "slight priority" to turn to the conversion of hearts. This means "fighting peacefully" but resolutely. Ultimately the Pope classified the problems as ethically, not technically. This is unfortunately based in the fact that the concept of human development is thought inadequately and mostly only in terms of material prosperity.

## 4. Concretions and guidelines

The Church itself should be a witness of justice. Therefore, the own behaviour, possessions and way of life must be subjected to a thorough examination.

Until the turn of the millennium the churches' investments lacked ethical criteria - at least for the Catholic Church. Only with the public pressure of a sensible society questions of ethics and sustainability has infiltrated their financial investments concepts. Pioneers were the religious orders and dioceses. The Central Committee of the German Catholics and the German Bishops' Conference finally approved in 2007 a handout on ethical investment. Not just returns, but a contribution to justice, peace and the integrity of creation should be connected. Three criteria have been set for ethical investments:

> "1. Does investment promote people's lives, the preservation of creation and international and intergenerational justice?
> 2. Does the instrument help poor people to receive concrete support in their efforts to improve living conditions?
> 3. Are companies financed whose products and manufacturing processes benefit people, the environment and the economies, particularly in developing and emerging countries?" (Hoffmann, 2015, p. 470)

Finally, in 2015 the German Bishops' Conference and the Central Committee of German Catholics jointly edited the guidelines "Invest ethically and sustainably". It is aimed to those people who are in charge of financial affairs in Catholic institutions and should help parishes, foundations, religious communities and associations to carry out their financial management ethically and sustainably. In addition to providing general guidance, the main part describes seven practical steps towards ethically sustainable investment. These steps were made to give a sign for credibility and transparency in the way how the Church deals with her money.

In recent years plenty of guidelines were compiled. This concerns also the Evangelical Church. Also plenty of guidelines about fair world trade, responsibility for creation and climate protection can be found. They are easily accessible on the websites of the particular institutions. Look for a general view: https://weltkirche.katholisch.de/Themen/Ethisches-Investment

# 5. A brief ecumenical view

A look beyond the (Catholic) Christian perspective may complement the perspective presented here.

## 5.1. Ecumenical initiatives

At its World Assembly 1983 in Vancouver, the World Council of Churches made peace, justice and the protection of creation to the goal of a conciliar process. The participants of all Christian churches shared the conviction that these three are the vital key topics for the future. They are deeply connected and must be addressed together.

This process found a Europe-specific form with the first Ecumenical Assembly in Basel in 1989. Since then, the three terms "peace - justice - preservation of creation" have become the centrepiece of a contemporary Christian commitment to the world.

Many initiatives have emerged from this, like the ecumenical grassroots movement "Kairos Europa" in Germany. It implements the international documents exemplary. For years there has been a network of groups and parishes. They are searching ways how our economic and development model can be fundamentally rebuilt. In addition to the three main topics, the focus was on the commitment to refugees. In ecumenical unity - also with Buddhists – they proclaim a certain statement. They reject an economic order based on excessive consumption and greed, which leads us to want to own more and more. (For current information: https://kairoseuropa.de/

Other communities, the "Kairos-Gemeinden", try to perceive the marginalised at their special locations and investigate where transformations must therefore begin. Other examples are the "anders wachsen" (grow differently) communities, which search exemplary for alternatives to current forms of life and business. Consumption will be oriented towards social and ecological criteria living in the sense of having enough.

So-called "Transformations-Gemeinden" (transformation communities) are working on similar topics. The ecumenical process takes up the keyword of a "great transformation", as it is also requested by the Scientific Advisory Board of the German Federal Government. However, criticism of the global capitalism of these projects is a bit weaker here.

### 5.2. Muslims and the waiver of interest

The main topic of the Muslims in the western countries is not the economy or the ecology, it is integration and the question of an European Islam. The focus is on religious and cultural identity. Therefore, one reads less about the common good on the homepages of the Islamic associations.

But Islam regulates human behaviour very concrete and therefore also gives instructions for economic behaviour. The main sources of Islam - the Quran and the Sunnah of the Prophet - provide guidelines for economic behaviour of a society. Justice plays an important role. For example, a certain allowance for KWh electricity or cubic meters of water can be obtained for each household. Public property includes public facilities such as mosques, schools, hospitals, which must not be privately owned. An Islamic state is supposed to pursue a fair distribution of wealth. Islam also strictly refuses the hoarding of money: "Those who devour interest should not look any different than someone who is seized by Satan and driven mad. This is because Muslims say that trade is the same as taking interest." (Al-Baqara 2, Aya 275)
Many Muslim economists criticise the dominant economic system of the West, which is imposed on other cultures. They call for a fundamentally different, Islamic economic order, which is discussed under the term "Islamic Economics". It is expressly based on norms and values from religion. Banks and interest rate play a particular role: According to the widespread view of Muslims, interest rate is the basic evil of Western economic systems.
The ban on interest is combined with the requirement to invest only in real existing values and prohibits business in pork, weapons, game of hazard or pornography. The prohibition of interest should be the supporting pillar of the Islamic economic system. Today,

these rules are melting with the western system, because certain sources and legal opinions - fatwas - allow the conclusion that the interpretation is not so clear. Moderate bank interest rates are therefore possible.

### 5.3. Jews and prophecy

The question of justice has become a difficult topic for Jews. Social justice is an ongoing program in Jewish history. Prophets have always demanded social, economic and environmental justness in the name of God but the trauma of the Holocaust has disrupted this clear effort. The discussion about a balance between the universal horizon and particular state security interests divides the society. The lack of justice in the Jewish Bible had clear consequences: namely the expulsion to Babylonian exile 2600 years ago.

The prophetic, first of all, is not seen politically or economically but in a suitable life according to Gods will. Justice is a particular attribute of God. So common good means doing justice to the wellbeing of all. Only a justice-oriented restructuring of Israeli society brings it closer to messianic arrival of God. However, many Jews conjure up the prophetic spirit that Israel has planted in as the greatest gift to the world. But now this prophetic element has become independent and emancipated from Jewish history.

Overall, it is worth taking a look at different religious and spiritual traditions. All have dignity and common good in mind and can inspire today's efforts for a good life for all people. In the competition for the common good, an interreligious dialogue could lead to new forms of connectedness and peaceful networking.

# 6. Conclusion

ECG tries to act on three levels. First the churches, as an enterprise like others, has to put into practice their own values and the values of the common good. Although they have to deal responsibly and economically with their assets, they may be less in direct economic competition and can therefore set a good example in terms of credibility. At the same time, churches can act on a political level as a cooperator for revision of a statue and an economic framework that is beneficial to the common good. And last but not least, they can, also with the educational institutions they maintain, work for a change in awareness and active engagement for the values of the common good.

Overall, I therefore see the special contribution of the churches less in the technical-instrumental area (balance sheet instruments), not in high competence in individual fields but in the field of awareness raising, networking of various initiatives and the encouragement of individual and committed groups. In contrast to NGOs, religions see themselves as communities that strive to shape all of life from the spiritual source of faith. Instead of taking a sectoral approach, religions shape a holistic view of the world. Ideas of transcendental salvation develop a high level of emotionality and motivation, not negative in fanaticism but positive in passionate commitment. The worldwide community character enables a face-to-face encounter of people in the context of model projects despite the globalised world. Global organisations, churches and religious communities can establish global connections comparatively easily and directly. The globalisation issues are given concrete faces. As a result, people experience the immediate and personal impact of their solidarity-based behaviour. The Brazilian dam project Belo Monte would never have been viewed so intensively critically in Austria if there were not a bishop from Austria in the middle of the Brazilian rainforest.

Religions' visions of the good life go beyond the earthly horizon. Therefore, it helps to be better able to bear the pressure of earthly urgency in a relaxed manner. Ultimately, the commitment to dignity and the common good can "only be found in the uniqueness of human nature: Man is not just the homo faber, who is working and struggling; he is not only the homo consumens, who is constantly chasing material needs; he is also the animal sociale that seeks community with man and nature, and the homo ludens et ridens that breathes the playful and creative freedom that makes him human." (Rosenberger, 2017, p. 323)

## 7. References

Deutsche Bischofskonferenz. (2010). Changing the world through investment? An aid to orientation on ethically-related investment. A study by the Group of Experts on "World Economy and Social Ethics", Bonn. Retrieved January 14, 2020, from https://www.dbk-shop.de/de/deutsche-bischofskonferenz/publikationen-der-wissenschaftlichen-arbeitsgruppe-fuer-weltkirchliche-aufgaben/studien-sachverstaendigengruppe-weltwirtschaft-sozialethik/changing-the-world-through-investment.html

Gabriel, I. (2017). Ökonomik – Theologie – Sozialethik. Divergenzen und Konvergenzen. In I. Gabriel, P.G. Kirchschläger, R. Sturn (Eds.), Eine Wirtschaft, die Leben fördert. Wirtschafts- und unternehmensethische Reflexionen im Anschluss an Papst Franziskus (pp. 23-49). Ostfildern: Schwabenverlag.

Hoffmann J. (2016). Ethisch-nachhaltig investieren mit DBK und ZdK, In P.-C. Chittilappilly (Eds), Horizonte gegenwärtiger Ethik (Festschrift für Josef Schuster SJ), pp.468-488, Freiburg: Herder.

Rosenberger M. (2012), Gut leben statt viel (ver-)brauchen. Schöpfungsethische Erwägungen, in: A. Findl-Ludescher, E. Langhammer, J. Panhofer (Eds), Gutes Leben - für alle? Theologisch-kritische Perspektiven auf einen aktuellen Sehnsuchtsbegriff, Wien: LITVerlag pp. 321-334.

Sedmak, C. (2017). "Die Würde des Menschen ist unantastbar". Zur Anwendung der katholischen Soziallehre. Regensburg: Pustet.

## 8. Abbreviations

EG      Francis. (2013). Evangelii Gaudium. Apostolic Exhortation. Rom. Retrieved January 14, 2020, from http://www.vatican.va/content/francesco/en/apost_exhortations/documents/papa-francesco_esortazione-ap_20131124_evangelii-gaudium.html

LS      Francis. (2015). Laudato Si. On Care for our Common Home. Rom. Retrieved January 14, 2020, from http://www.vatican.va/content/francesco/en/encyclicals/documents/papa-francesco_20150524_enciclica-laudato-si.html

GS      Paul VI. (Ed.). (1965). Gaudium et Spes. Pastoral Constitution of the Church in the modern World. Rom, Retrieved January 14, 2020, from http://www.vatican.va/archive/hist_councils/ii_vatican_council/documents/vat-ii_const_19651207_gaudium-et-spes_en.html

CV      Benedict XVI. (2009) Caritas in Veritate. Rom, Retrieved January 14, 2020, from http://www.vatican.va/content/benedict-xvi/en/encyclicals/documents/hf_ben-xvi_enc_20090629_caritas-in-veritate.html

LC      Congregation for the Doctrine of the Faith (Eds.). (1986). Instruction on Christian Freedom and Liberation "The truth makes us free", Rom, Retrieved January 14, 2020, from http://www.vatican.va/roman_curia/congregations/cfaith/documents/rc_con_cfaith_doc_19860322_freedom-liberation_en.html

# Spreading it – The Conference Design of the first international ECG (Economy of the Common Good) conference in Bremen

*Christian Harant*

## 1. Introduction

The papers were selected, the shortlist of keynotes was ready and since this was the first international conference of the ECG.

Some days after a rough briefing on the state of the project, I presented a short presentation that had one thing in mind: to shift viewpoints.

From the "problem" of how to merge the two days with two completely different groups of audience, the focus switched to the chances, when bringing those two groups together. Seeing it as a benefit to mix groups and letting them interact.

Another point was to shift from classical conference with its well known rituals to a science conference being the place of inspiring encounters. New fields of research could be discovered and the mutual enhancement of users and theory should find enough time and space.

All the team members went with the idea, to make a difference. The openness and trust of the team combined with an enormous amount of work made this conference work.

It was a great opportunity for a young field of research that made a different approach to a scientific conference possible. The conference was design to support and establish "mental sustainability" as an expression of ECG.

I use the term "mental sustainability" referring to Bernd Fittkau, who contributed an approach to a different kind of thinking in his speech as an indispensible way for changing economy as it is today.

# 2. Presumptions behind the Conference Design

### 2.1 To learn means to meet the unexpected

When entering a classical research conference you may find a kind of pattern that constantly reoccurs. Registration - paper presentation in frontal setting - coffee breaks and lunch/ dinner are the occasions to make contacts – windup.

For the audience that usually means to sit in rows, watch and listen to paper presentations for hours.

This all resembles to some extent the well-known school and university learning settings. At least in most schools in the world. We all learned implicitly that this symbolizes hierarchy: somebody in the front is the one who knows, the others are meant to be learning. We are used to that and therefore we don't question it. This seems to mark a constant cultural pattern that often hinders us to learn.
A change of setting opens up a field of behaviour with more opportunities to interact and learn by dialogue.

### 2.2 Change begins on the level of questioning habits and customs.

Content is much easier subject to change than are the habits shown at a scientific conference.

If scientific conferences serve primarily as entry point to being published in scientific magazines, this presumption limits the possibilities that come with it to, of course, being published.

This was to be altered in the context of ECG going scientific.

### 2.3 A conference is a pivoting point of communication for people

The process does not stop at the end of the conference. It sets a starting point and is able to impact on the ECG community even after the conference is.

A presumption that strongly resonated in the conference team and made decisions possible to get off the beaten tracks.

*2.4 Academically correct publications and different ways of interaction can be integrated*

ECG is a critical movement that aims to rethink economic habits in theory and application. So we headed for a scientific research conference that integrates preconditions of acknowledgement in the scientific community AND learning in a profound way that leaves well known academic habits behind.

As it turned out both intentions can be integrated: academically correct publications AND new ways of interaction that enable inspiring insights.

This integrative concept could be an expression of all alternative economic approaches. Even in the field of classical conferences it opens up new ways of exchange and at the ECGPW-2019 it set a landmark.

## 3. Aims that led to the design of ECGPW-2019

Understanding the assumptions to a different approach, aims were identified that should be focused during he conference:

- to bring ECG-science to the scientific field

- a conference that inspires, enables new fields of research and consequently leads to exchange and non-hierarchical encounters to enable new insights.

- connecting the field of application with the scientific community to mutually profit form the different needs and perspectives

- providing more than the professional elaboration and sharing of knowledge – try out new ways of encounter and exchange.

- making diversity a resource by inviting different perspectives and give the opportunity to make them visible

- providing productive encounters and discussions as part of the schedule- not only in breaks

- forming a conference that provides an experience what a different kind of scientific culture could mean to all of us

## 5. Bringing it to live

To accomplish a complex conference design like this needs a lot of skills, knowledge and dedication. To bring the ideas and presumptions of this concept to life needs a strong and dedicated team.

And it found very good conditions for a high quality outcome due to the the host "Hochschule Bremen" and the Institute…

The core elements of the conference design:

- Introduction by a board of keynote speakers
  - The first occasion that addressed the main topics of the conference. The audience contributed being part of a "fishbowl" together with the speakers.

- ECG Science Talks
  - The core of the paper presentations.
  - Topics were arranged by similarity in parallel sessions.
  - The setting was designed to enable dialogues. After short presentations the audience was invited to discuss.
  - Keynotes that address main topics of the event

- Large Group formats combined with Keynotes
  - To bring together applicants, activists and scientists a world café was arranged to enable working on questions both groups would benefit of.

- Good documentation to seed ideas and thoughts for new topics of research

## 6. Outlook

The conference ECGPW-2019 was meant as a prototype - forming a field of mutual exchange, integrating perspectives, learning by encounters and dialogues. It represented an eco2system connecting economy and ecology.

Bringing science, users and activists together could be a model for future conferences. To make this kind of working together a habit, we need to form a new field that supports change. According the voices of participants the conference contributed to new ways of thinking and acting for the ECG movement.

## 7. References (mostly in German)

Foerster, H. v. (2001): Wahrheit ist die Erfindung eines Lügners. Heidelberg: Carl Auer

Geißlinger H. (1999): Überfälle auf die Wirklichkeit. Heidelberg: Carl Auer

Geißlinger H., Raab S. (2007): Strategische Inszenierung. Heidelberg: Carl Auer

Hüther G. (2011): Was wir sind und was wir sein könnten. Frankfurt a.M.: Fischer

Hüther G. (2016): Mit Freude lernen ein Leben lang. Göttingen: Vandenhoek & Ruprecht

Lotter W. (2018): Innovation. Hamburg: Edition Körber

Papanek V. (1971): Design for the real World. London: Thames and Hudson

Scharmer, C. O. (2007): Theorie U. Heidelberg: Carl Auer

Simon, F. B. (2009): Einführung in Systemtheorie und Konstruktivismus. Heidelberg: Carl Auer

# Conference Program

## Thursday, 28th November 2019
*Venue: Graduate and Professional School, Event Hall*

| | | |
|---|---|---|
| 17:30 | **Arrival & Registration** | |
| 18:00 | **Conference Opening** | |
| | Welcome | Prof. Dr. Tim Goydke<br>*Dean, School of Graduate and Professional Studies,*<br>*City University of Applied Sciences Bremen* |
| | | Prof. Dr. h.c. Günther Koch<br>*Chairman, Research Council of the Economy for the Common Good* |
| | Introduction | Dr. Christian Harant<br>*Moderator* |
| 18:15 | **Opening Keynotes** | Christian Felber<br>*ECG Founder, Author, Lecturer* |
| | | Dr. J. Daniel Dahm<br>*World Future Council* |
| 18:45 | **Panel Discussion / Fishbowl** | |
| | Moderator | Dr. Christian Harant |
| 20:00 | **Closing Remarks** | |
| 20:15 | **Reception** | |

## Friday, 29th November 2019
*Venue: Graduate and Professional School, Event Hall*

| | | |
|---|---|---|
| 09:00 | **Registration** | |
| 09:30 | **Introductory Notes** | Dr. Christian Harant |
| 09:40 | **Keynote** | Prof. Dr. Silja Graupe, President, Cusanus Hochschule |
| 10:25 | **Parallel Sessions** | |

**ECG Science Talk 1: Policy Impact – Local, National, Global**

*"Modern Monetary Theory and the Public Purpose"*
Dirk H. Ehnts (Technical University Chemnitz) and Maurice Höfgen (Pufendorf-Gesell-schaft e.V./ Pluralism in Economics Maastricht)

*"The return of Universal Welfare State-Free public services and the making of new business: the comparative case studies of Thailand, Estonia and Finland"*
Sustarum Thaamaboosadee (Thammasat University)

*"Living up to the Universal Social Contract: A potential route towards the Economy of the Common Good?"*
*Elly Rijnierse (ECG NL / Asterope Consultancy)*

*"Artificial Intelligence, the Spare Time Rebound Effect and How the ECG Would Avoid It"*
Wolfgang Ertel (University of Applied Sciences Ravensburg-Weingarten)

**ECG Science Talk 2: ECG Matrix – Implementation and Impact**

*"Large multinational companies and their orientation towards the common good. An empirical insight into chances and barriers"*
Josefa Kny (Europe University Flensburg)

*"Integral Approach to deal with obstacles during an ECG implementation"*
Matthias Rausch and Jens Nitsche (Yellow Birds Consulting)

*"The ECG Matrix as a Tool for Corporate Sustainability Management"*
Hendrik Lambrecht, Claus Lang-Koetz, Felix Krebber (Pforzheim University of Applied Sciences)

*"The Common Good Approach in Entrepreneurial Practice"*
Jasmin Wiefek (Institute for Advanced Sustainability Studies e.V. (IASS) Potsdam & Freie Universität Berlin)

12:25   *Lunch Break*

**13:35   Parallel Sessions**

**ECG Science Talk 3: Workshop on ECG in Higher Education and Research**

Workshop Input:
-   Tim Goydke (City University of Applied Sciences Bremen)
-   Mercè Carreras-Solanas (University of Barcelona)
-   Guenther Jedliczka, Carina Kamptner and Petra Isepp (AEMS Summer School)
-   Johanna Stöhr, Christian Herzig, Maren Busch (Kassel University)
-   Robert Mende-Kremnitzer (University of Applied Sciences Wiener Neustadt)

### ECG Science Talk 4: Linking ECG to Connecting/Alternative Concepts

*"Linking the common good balance sheet to the ISO 14.001:2015 Environmental management systems"*
Nathali Jänicke (Jade Hochschule)

*"ECG trumps the Red Queen"*
Miquel Banchs-Piqué (University of Portsmouth)

*"Contributions to Knowledge-Based Development from the Commons Theory"*
Maria Angelica Jung Marques, Federal University of Santa Catarina, Jamile Sabatini Marques, University of Sao Paulo, Blanca C. Garcia, El Colegio de la Frontera Norte - COLEF, Tatiana Tucunduva Philippi Cortese, UNINOVE / IEA USP, Eduardo Costa, Federal University of Santa Catarina

*"Is Pope Francis an Undercover Agent of the Economy for the Common Good?"*
Johannes Panhofer (Innsbruck University)

15:35    *Coffee Break*

**16:05    Parallel Sessions**

### ECG Science Talk 5: ECG Legal Framework

*„Die Gemeinwohl-Bilanz 5.0 im Lichte der gesetzlichen Berichtspflicht nach dem deutschen CSR-Richtlinien-Umsetzungsgesetz (CSR-RUG)"*
Stefanie Deinert

*"The interaction between competition law and the Economy of the Common Good"*
Lydia Scholz (City University of Applied Sciences Bremen)

*"Economy for the Common Good (ECG) and Taxation"*
Vera de Hesselle (City University of Applied Sciences Bremen)

### ECG Science Talk 6: From Theory to Practice

*"Process Design and Transformation towards Commoning"*
Christian Stary (Johannes Keppler University Linz)

*"Will common good balancing set the world on fire? Competition(s) for common good as an additional tool for accelerating a transition"*
Stefan Schwaderlapp

*"Economic Development, Social Networks and Well-Being: An Alternative Approach"*
Chakib Bourayou (SOAS, University of London), Phillippe Gozdawa (University of Buckingham)

*"Is working for an Economy for the Common Good organisation beneficial for workers' health and job satisfaction? A propensity score matching analysis"*
Laia Ollé-Espluga, Johanna Muckenhuber and Markus Hadler (University of Graz)

**18:05** **Ambassadors Circle – Results from the Sessions / Wrap-up**

**18:30** **Evening Thoughts**
*"Mental sustainability: from need to value orientation - ... and back. How can we steer our companies into a humane future? - Using the example of the ECG"* (German with translation)
Bernd Fittkau

**18:45** **Science goes Social**


# Saturday, 30th November 2019
*Venue: Graduate and Professional School, Event Hall*

**09:30** **Einführung/Introduction: Wissenschaft für die Praxis / Science for the Real World**

**09:40** **Keynote:**

**10:10** **Konferenzbericht / Conference Insights**

**10:40** **ECG Forum / World Café**

**12:55** **Mittagspause / Lunch Break**

**13:55** **Keynote:**

**14:55** **Fishbowl: Sharing Perspectives**

**15:30** **Closing Remarks**

# Authors

**Eduardo Costa**
Federal University of Santa Catarina, UFSC - Postgraduate Program in Engineering and Knowledge Management – EGC, Brazil

**J. Daniel Dahm**
Founder, United Sustainability Group; Spokesperson "Ecosystem Restoration", World Future Council; Member, German Association of the Club of Rome, Germany

**Anna Deparnay-Grunenberg**
Member of the European Parliament, The Greens / EFA Group, Belgium

**Blanca C. Garcia**
KBD Assoc. Prof., El Colegio de la Frontera Norte - COLEF, Mexico

**Bernd Fittkau**
Humanistic psychologist, emeritus professor for Educational Psychology, Germany

**Tim Thomas Goydke**
Professor and Dean, School of Graduate and Professional Studies, Hochschule Bremen - City University of Applied Sciences, Germany

**Christian Harant**
Design and development consultant, Austria

**Nathali Tatjana Jänicke**
Professor at Jade Hochschule, Campus Wilhelmshaven, Faculty of Business Administration and Management, Germany

**Maria Angelica Jung Marques**
Federal University of Santa Catarina, UFSC - Postgraduate Program in Engineering and Knowledge Management – EGC, Brazil

**Günther Koch**
Chairman, Research Council of the Economy for the Common Good, Austria

**Bianca Llerandi**
Local parliamentary assistant in the constituency office of MEP Anna Deparnay-Grunenberg, Germany

**Johannes Panhofer**
Lecturer, Institut for Practical Theology, Innsbruck University, Austria

**Elly Rijnierse**
Associated with the Sustainability Research Group of the University of Humanistic Studies, Economy for the Common Good Science-Hub NL, Netherlands

**Jamile Sabatini Marques**
Institute of Advanced Studies, University of Sao Paulo, Brazil

**Christian Stary**
Head and full professor of Business Informatics-Communications Engineering, JKU Knowledge Management Competence Centre, Johannes Kepler University in Linz, Austria

**Tatiana Tucunduva Philippi Cortese**
Master Program in Smart and Sustainable Cities at UNINOVE and researcher at IEA USP, Brazil

Zeitfracht Medien GmbH
Ferdinand-Jühlke-Straße 7
99095 Erfurt, Deutschland
produktsicherheit@kolibri360.de